T0299640

Louisa Clarke works with leaders and high-performing teams from some of the world's best companies. An experienced facilitator and qualified coach with an outstanding new-business track record, Louisa is a Managing Partner at The Caffeine Partnership – a strategic consultancy that stimulates growth through brand strategy, customer experience and employee experience. She regularly coaches, consults and trains leaders and teams around the world on business development and communication. A former Great Britain junior international rower and current masters rower, she brings a competitive track record to motivate people under pressure, understanding the power of teamwork and what's required to win. www.thisiscaffeine.com

THE
WORK
SMARTER
GUIDE TO
PRESENTING

Louisa Clarke
Series Editor David Kean

A How To book

ROBINSON

ROBINSON

First published in Great Britain in 2024
by Robinson.

10 9 8 7 6 5 4 3 2 1

A CIP catalogue record for this book
is available from the British Library.

ISBN: 978-1-47214-883-4

Typeset in Sentinel and Scala Sans
by Ian Hughes.

Printed and bound in Great Britain by Clays
Ltd, Elcograf S.p.A.

Papers used by Robinson are from well-
managed forests and other responsible
sources.

Robinson
An imprint of
Little, Brown Book Group
Carmelite House
50 Victoria Embankment
London EC4Y 0DZ

An Hachette UK Company
www.hachette.co.uk

www.littlebrown.co.uk

How To Books are published by
Robinson, an imprint of Little, Brown
Book Group. We welcome proposals
from authors who have first-hand
experience of their subjects. Please set
out the aims of your book, its target
market and its suggested contents in an
email to howto@littlebrown.co.uk.

To Hannah – LSL forever!

Contents

Introduction

'There are always three speeches for every one you actually give. The one you prepared, the one you gave and the one you wish you gave.'
DALE CARNEGIE,
AUTHOR, *HOW TO WIN FRIENDS AND INFLUENCE PEOPLE*

There's a piece of research which reveals that the top fear in life is presenting in public.[1] In second place, death. Apparently, most people would rather die than talk to an audience.

Fear of speaking in public is called 'glossophobia'. The term comes from the Greek words *glossa* (tongue) and *phobos* (dread or fear). If you've ever been asked to make a presentation, and it's something that you don't regularly do, you'll be familiar with the visceral feeling that sweeps through your body and mind at the thought of it. Racing heartbeat, sweaty palms, butterflies in your stomach, mind racing at the sheer horror of it. No wonder that, for a fleeting moment, peaceful oblivion feels more appealing.

It doesn't have to be this way.

It is possible to stand up and give a presentation, speech, lesson or vote of thanks in a way that captures your audience's attention. One that actually makes them think, feel or do something as a result. All without giving you sleepless nights and raging anxiety in anticipation.

Having good, even great, presentation skills is not out of reach. It's not the God-given gift of a few lucky people. *Everyone* can improve

---

[1] R. H. Bruskin Associate's American Fears study, which first appeared in the *Sunday Times*.

their communication (which is essentially what presentation skills are) and, by doing so, remove the fear factor. All it takes is some practice.

But where to start? Right here. This book is a practical guide that gets straight to the point with top tips, tools and techniques to help you create and deliver presentations that you'll enjoy giving and that your audience will want to hear. And by doing so, you'll find that being able to communicate effectively will accelerate both your confidence and your career. I truly believe that the ability to give great presentations – and gain a reputation for doing so – is the quickest way to stand out from your peers and your competitors.

And it's not just me that believes this – the world's most famous financier, Warren Buffett, said:

> I don't have my diploma from the University of Nebraska hanging on my office wall, and I don't have my diploma from Columbia up there either – but I do have my Dale Carnegie graduation certificate proudly displayed. That $100 course on effective speaking gave me the most important degree I have.

Great presentation skills open doors to opportunities: present your ideas well and they are more likely to be bought. Give a compelling pitch presentation and you will beat your competition, win new revenues and build your business. Communicate clearly and you will motivate your team or your students. You may end up earning your living from speaking in public. But even if you have no ambition to be the Sheryl Sandberg of your industry and only picked up this book because you hate presenting but can no longer avoid it, congratulations. You've taken the first step in taking a smarter approach to becoming a better presenter. Your audience will thank you and, in the future, you will be spared unnecessary angst. Let's get to it!

1.
Before we begin

A CAUTIONARY TALE

Let's start by casting your mind back to the worst presentation you've ever given.

Chances are you didn't have to think too long before the painful memory of a disastrous performance rose to the surface. These things stay with us.

Mine was over twenty years ago. I had been invited to a multi-agency 'Loop Team' meeting – leaders from different marketing disciplines brought together to share best practice and collaborate in service of our mutual multinational client.

I can't remember what my presentation was about. I have no recollection of rehearsing. But I remember that, just before I stepped up to the lectern, the Loop Team leader took me aside and said, 'We need more energy. Be Dolly Parton.'

I trust you are familiar with the iconic Dolly. If you are unfamiliar with her work, pause and Google her. For those who haven't met me, simply imagine the total, polar opposite of everything Dolly Parton epitomises.

If Dolly Parton danced around the stage, I walked slowly. If she spoke with a light trill and a girlish laugh, I was tonally similar to the speaking clock. If she lit up the audience's hearts and minds with her vivacity, I had thirty PowerPoint slides and was damn well going to use them.

Put simply, there was a huge, gaping, insurmountable void between the bubbly, vivacious, teeth-and-eyes personality of the iconic Ms. Parton and me, age twenty-eight.

So, when I heard that direction from stage left, I didn't do what any normal person would do, which would have been to smile, nod and then do my own thing, confident that I had rehearsed and was ready.

No, I didn't do that. Turned out I wasn't a normal person. And I'm not sure I had rehearsed. I was an idiot people-pleaser back then. I did what I was told.

At this point your imagination is probably ahead of reality. It wasn't so bad that I got up and did my presentation through the medium of song, with some added dancing for good measure. I didn't do a Dolly impression. The audience wasn't totally cringing and I didn't totally die of shame.

However, I did latch onto the word 'energy' from the brief, and I took that energy and I turned it into speed. Rather than demonstrating energy through a dynamic and engaging performance, I raced through my slides at record pace. I gabbled, I barely drew breath; I raced on and on, at warp speed, my speech speeding up, my oxygen running out. And when I got to the last slide, I practically ran off stage, panting.

In the dark moments afterwards someone from the audience came up to me and said, 'You couldn't wait for that to end, could you?'

So much for the content that I'd spent hours scripting and the slides that I'd spent days finessing. If his overriding impression of my presentation was 'GET ME OUT OF HERE!', then the rest of the audience probably took that away too. If they thought of me at all, it wasn't my key messages that resonated. It was the memory of a manic race through thirty slides in five minutes delivered by a wide-eyed woman vibrating with stress.

The experience served a purpose: to remind me of the need to prepare, practice and improve so that now – irony – I help others avoid my fate through presentation and pitch coaching.

The moral of my cautionary tale is that you don't have to do what you're told. People give unsolicited advice. You have to decide what's *helpful*. Trust your instinct. My instinct knew that the Dolly Parton brief was totally incongruous with who I am, and yet I overrode that instinct. With less than spectacular results. To follow the approach in this book won't require you to pretend to be someone you're not. Instead, it will give you tools and techniques that will remove any terror you may have, save you time and make the whole experience of presenting in public easier and more enjoyable. And, because we all enjoy a bit of schadenfreude (the pleasure derived from another person's misfortune), I share some more cautionary tales throughout the book. So you can comfort yourself with the thought, *at least I won't be as bad as that* . . .

FIRST THINGS FIRST – GET OVER YOURSELF

Over the years, I've worked with senior women and men responsible for multimillion-pound budgets and teams of hundreds of people who spend their working lives at a cracking pace. Their decisions make the difference between organisational success or failure.

These people seem uber-confident, unruffled and experienced, and yet I cannot tell you how many of them say to me: 'I hate presenting. I really hate it.' Despite this proclamation, these *übermensch* will do all they can to avoid doing anything that might help them become better. They won't write a script; they won't be disciplined or clear about what key message they want to get across; and they won't, God forbid, rehearse. Instead, they rock up to an internal meeting, town hall or even a keynote speech and 'wing it' – speaking off the cuff (which is code for rambling on), fidgeting and pacing the stage (because they think they'll look like Steve Jobs – they don't), running on too long and boring their audience to tears. Harsh but, unfortunately, true.

One of my clients epitomised this approach. He said, 'I hate presenting. But I won't do anything to prepare myself to be better at it because if I do nothing, then at least I can blame my bad performance on the fact that I didn't rehearse.' There's a kind of logic to this but why, in a world that encourages us to 'be our best selves' and where we take the rest of our professional development so seriously, do we allow ourselves to be so mediocre when it comes to presenting?

My response to this client and to every other client who comes up with this approach is 'Get over yourself.' It's a message that I first told myself when, like my clients, I could spend hours twisting my thoughts into mental knots about why I was so bad at something and still do nothing to improve my performance. The reality is either you choose to do what it takes to improve or shut up with the excuses. As my son frequently says to me, 'No one cares.'

Well, that's not entirely true. I care.

I care because I've seen the transformation of individuals and businesses as they get out of old, ineffectual habits to enjoy vastly improved results by adopting a different approach to presenting. I care because I hate to see brilliance go to waste as great ideas are diluted or lost in a fog of badly presented, over-complex and instantly forgettable charts. I care that people are working stupid hours because they didn't get organised the moment the brief or the meeting invitation pinged into the inbox.

Here are three tips to make you care too:

1. As Yoda said, 'Do or do not. There is no "try".'
Presenting well is really only about one thing. Practice. If you're not 100 per cent committed to practising (AKA rehearsal) then don't bother. I can be incredibly eloquent in my head, as I lie in bed, imagining myself on stage wowing the audience, but I know that unless I do all the hard work of planning, preparing and *rehearsing* (which means speaking out loud not just running through your words silently in your head), that image will remain what it is – a dream.

2. Don't do it all at the last minute.

A statement from the department of the bleeding obvious perhaps, but piss-poor time management is probably the biggest contributor to piss-poor presentations. Many of us love the adrenaline of the looming deadline but wasting between 20 and 50 per cent of the time available by procrastinating instead of getting cracking immediately doesn't add a gritty edge of brinkmanship to your presentation, it just means you're on the back foot. Get on with it ASAP and aim to finish – rehearsals and all – 24 hours before the day of delivery. Imagine that – a good night's sleep the night before you make your presentation. It can be done and it makes a HUGE difference to your energy and attitude on the day.

3. Less is more.

We love to think our audience is soaking up our words like a sponge, absorbing and remembering every line of our incisive thoughts. Yet we know from our own listening habits that this simply isn't the case. Our brains can only remember so much. So limit the number of key points you want to make.

A good discipline is for every presenter to write down the one thing the audience *must* remember by the time that presenter sits down. Write that point on a standard-sized Post-it note in normal-sized handwriting – this forces people to focus on what's important. It stops presenters waffling. It's a self-editing tool to sharpen your presentation and it ensures that each section of the presentation has a point. Keep the main thing the main thing. What are you asking the audience to think, feel, do? I'll remind you of the importance of these three themes throughout the book – they focus the mind on the audience, rather than on ourselves. And that's liberating.

A QUICK NOTE ON CONFIDENCE

'All the great speakers were bad speakers at first.'
RALPH WALDO EMERSON

Before every presentation skills training workshop I run, I distribute a short questionnaire to the participants. One of the questions I ask is, 'What do you want to get from the workshop?', and nine times out of ten the answer is: 'More confidence.'

Everyone will have a different view on what 'confidence' looks and feels like, but if we look at the dictionary definition it is 'the feeling or belief that one can have faith in or rely on someone or something'. If we are confident in our presentation skills, then we remove angst and anxiety because we know we can rely on ourselves. We know we can do a good job.

Confidence usually grows by doing things a bit differently on a daily basis, by pushing yourself out of your comfort zone and living to tell the tale. Here we enter the zone of 'personal growth'. As the actor Donald Glover said, 'If it makes you nervous, you're doing it right.'

To that end, take every opportunity you can to speak, to speak up and to speak out. Say yes to giving presentations. Say yes to 'saying a few words' at the start of a meeting. But do yourself and your audience a favour and prepare and practise. Get a reputation for being concise and compelling rather than rambling and verbose.

A MERCIFULLY BRIEF LOOK AT HOW THE BRAIN WORKS (AND WHY THIS IS IMPORTANT)

Because you're reading this book, I assume you're committed to delivering a great presentation. You're up for putting the time in to make it the best you can, but you're keen to get some shortcuts that can positively improve the impact you'll make. The last thing you probably want to read now is a couple of pages on how the brain functions. What's the point? Well, bear with me because (a) I promise this is a short bit; and (b) it is relevant to how we communicate and – vitally – how our audience retains information.

THE SCIENCE BIT

Massive caveat, I am no scientist, so this is an incredibly top line and broad-brush stroke (yet fact-checked) look at how the brain works. It's useful to know because how the brain functions has relevance to how we communicate.

The three main areas of the brain are the cerebrum, the cerebellum and the brain stem.

1. Cerebrum

When we imagine a picture of the brain, that wrinkled and compact rounded shape, we're thinking of the cerebrum. Its hills (gyri) and valleys (sulci) account for approximately 85 per cent of total brain volume and it controls functions such as speech, reasoning and emotion as well as sight, hearing and touch.

2. Cerebellum

Accounting for only 10 per cent of brain mass and neatly tucked away is the cerebellum, which is integral for motor control as well as maintaining balance and posture. Small but powerful, this 'little brain' is responsible for virtually all physical movement.

3. Brain stem

Connecting both the cerebrum and cerebellum to the spinal cord is the brain stem, which relays their messages and instructions throughout the body. It acts as a communication hub and also controls automatic functions such as breathing, temperature, digestion, swallowing and sleep cycles.

WHY IS THIS IMPORTANT?

The cerebrum is split into two halves, or hemispheres, which non-scientists (like me) refer to as the *left* and *right* sides of the brain.

Very broadly speaking, the left side of the brain is responsible for reasoning, logic, pattern creation, language and numerical skills. On the right side resides creativity, imagination, the senses, intuition and spatial awareness. For example, if you write a musical composition using notes on paper, you're using the left side of your brain (because sheet music uses precise logical symbols to denote pitch, rhythm, tempo, phrasing, etc.), but when you listen to music, you experience it in the right side of the brain. So the music stirs your emotions and evokes memories and images.

When we're preparing presentations, most of the time we focus on appealing to the left side of the brain. We over-index on facts, data, charts and information. We want to show our expertise, we want to demonstrate rational thinking and logic. But the two sides don't operate in isolation, they are constantly communicating through the corpus callosum, a collection of nerve fibres that links the two halves, so that we're able to engage both hemispheres simultaneously.

In layman's terms, the implication for our presentations is this – if we have a presentation that is too 'left-brain' focused, our right hemisphere starts to play up. Our mind goes for a wander. We stop concentrating on all those overwhelming facts and figures and get distracted by thoughts of what we're having for dinner or start thinking about our next holiday, because our right brain is being starved of the stimulus it needs. So it creates a stimulus to keep it occupied and entertained.

Similarly, if we are faced with a business presentation that is high on abstract concepts but with no grounding in reality, a presentation that is all show and bluster, our brains start craving some proof points, for something tangible to hold onto – like facts.

Importantly, it's not one side of the brain at the expense of the other. What we ideally want for our presentations is to appeal to *both* sides of the brain. That way, we keep our audience's attention for longer and limit the potential for their minds to wander. And, crucially, we help the brain to hold onto information in the memory. For surely, if we are going to the bother of creating and delivering a presentation, we want people to remember it.

HOW MEMORY WORKS

Memory is a highly complex process and, put simply, it depends on three stages:

1. Encoding: where we assess the information's importance and decide whether it is worth keeping or not

2. Storing: keeping the information ready to be available when needed

3. Recalling: how we retrieve information – this is what we experience as 'remembering'

Our brains are continually evaluating whether the information we receive is relevant or significant enough to hold onto. If we're in a situation where we need to recall a telephone number or we've asked for directions, we use our short-term memory and then forget the information when it is no longer needed. But if we decide that, actually, we will need to use those directions again, we start to employ our long-term memory, which occurs in the hippocampus. The hippocampus is an area of the temporal lobe – part of the brain that sits, appropriately, behind the ears – that has the capacity to store a large collection of information for a long time. If we decide that we are going to memorise our entire speech for an upcoming presentation, then we'll be putting our long-term memory to work. And if we are going to present something the audience feels is of great significance and worth remembering, they will be doing this too.

Furthermore, there are 'triggers' that an audience will respond to that will greatly increase the likelihood of our presentation ending up in their long-term memory. For example, when they recognise information as *significant,* when it provokes *emotional reactions* (both joyful and traumatic) and when the story is *compelling.* If you think back to a presentation that you remember from years ago, chances are it ticked the boxes for one or more of these triggers. If I think back over the course of my career, I have listened to thousands of presentations and speeches at company events and off-site strategy sessions. What do I recall? An 'overcoming all odds' motivational talk from Mark Woods, the Paralympic gold medal-winning swimmer, that was *emotive* and *compelling.* A rousing presentation on 'The Golden Rules of Pitching' by business development guru David Kean – because at the time the agency where I was working was failing to follow many of them, which was *significant.* A speech on the impact of climate change by Greta Thunberg was both emotive and traumatic. I'm still having nightmares about those polar bears.

So that's the goal – to use both sides of the brain to create a presentation that feeds the needs of the rational and the emotional hemispheres of your audience's brains *and* which is so compelling that something of what you said remains in their heads for years to come. Don't be disappointed if they don't remember every single syllable; no one is going to remember every word, however amazing you are. Even famous orators get misremembered and misquoted. It is enough that they were moved and persuaded enough to recall your message when they forgot everyone else's.

Let's look at how to do it.

PRIME PRESENTATIONS – AN ACRONYM FOR PRESENTATION SUCCESS

The dictionary definition of 'prime' is: 'of the best possible quality'. Which seems like a good starting point for an acronym that will help you prepare, plan and deliver your presentation.

The five areas of focus for the remainder of this book are:

Planning – the necessary forward thinking and preparation that will help you be your best on the day

Reason – why you're there in the first place

Impact – delivering a memorable – for the right reasons – and distinctive presentation to be proud of

Mission – what you want to accomplish with your presentation. 'Not making a fool of myself' is not a mission

Energy – dealing with nerves, warming up properly and doing all you can to direct the inevitable butterflies in the stomach and racing heart to serve you and not sabotage you

Before you even fire up your laptop or PC, before you pick up a pen and start scribbling, take the time to run through these five points and, I guarantee, your audience will thank you.

2.
Planning

'If it is a 10-minute speech it takes me all of two weeks. If it is a half-hour speech, it takes me a week. And if I can talk for as long as I want to, it requires no preparation at all.'
WOODROW WILSON ON SPEECHWRITING

Get the planning right and success follows. It's like exam prep. If you go into the examination hall having done no revision, no test papers and are just relying on your amazing brainpower then, speaking from experience, you're unlikely to ace your A-levels.

Yes, there are always those people who scrape through their exams swearing blind they have done no work. But, either way, there will always be that nagging feeling that makes you wonder what grade could you have got if you had done your homework, revised and done those test papers instead of staring out the window and watching YouTube videos in the name of research?

THE AUDIENCE
Let's start with the basics.

WHO AM I SPEAKING TO?
Your first job is to find out as much as possible about your audience. When you're speaking to a big group of people (a conference or a lecture) it's likely that you'll only get broad background information, such as are they young adults or middle-aged? Are they experienced leaders or are they a new graduate cohort? When you're speaking to only a few people (e.g., a board of directors, a committee, your class

at school), then it should be easier to get more detailed, personal information.

Here is a checklist of questions to ask:

- How many people will there be?
- What do they want to know? (You're there for a reason – what is it?)
- What age group are they?
- Is it a diverse group of people or does it skew to a particular demographic?
- What is the 'house style'? Is it a corporate organisation or is it a more casual environment?
- How long do they want you to speak?

WHY AM I TALKING?

This links to the question you've asked about the audience, 'What do they need to know'? What is your overall objective for your presentation? Can you crystallise this to one line? Too often we create a brief for ourselves that is too broad and end up adding more and more content so that we lose sight of the key thing we want to communicate.

Essentially, there are only three things that will happen to your audience when you present. **You will make them *think* something, you will make them *feel* something and you will make them *do* something.** If you are clear on what you want them to think, feel and do, you can create a presentation with that purpose in mind. If you are not clear, then they will think, feel, do something anyway but it may be they think that was a waste of time, they feel annoyed with you and they do nothing. Or they do tell their colleagues what a terrible presentation they've just sat through. Avoiding that outcome is why you are reading this book.

If you do nothing else, start with these three questions. I've given some examples of how you might answer them.

What do I want them to *think*?
- That I can solve their problem
- That I have done my research and know my stuff
- That I have a compelling argument
- That I have changed their mind
- That I have given them some new information
- That I am the best person, or we are the best company, to help them

What do I want them to *feel*?
- Excited – about the possibilities I've outlined
- Motivated – to take action
- Scared – something needs to be done
- Emotional – I want to make them cry; I want to make them laugh
- Reassured – I'm the right person for this
- Entertained – they had a great time

What do I want them to *do*?
- Sign a contract to work with me/my company
- Buy my book
- Commission me for a project
- Take action – join a group, take up a cause, do something *specific*
- Introduce me to another company/ contact
- Recommend me
- Give me a standing ovation

WHERE AM I GIVING THE PRESENTATION?

Here are some of the most common options:

THE BIG STAGE

This could be a corporate conference, a TedX Talk, a charity event or a festival. Anywhere that is a multimedia event with multiple speakers, a production team (even if that's just you and an assistant) and a large audience.

In this scenario, there's no way you can just rock up on the day and give your speech or presentation with no advance preparation. Any good event producer will have factored in:

- rehearsal time to run through what you're going to say
- the logistics of where you are in the running order
- how you get on and off the stage (nothing dents the confidence more than tripping up on the steps up to the stage)
- whether you have a lectern and mic or a lapel mic so you can roam the stage.

Big corporate presentations on stage often have a teleprompter – also known by the brand name 'Autocue' (which has become a generic, like 'Hoover') – a device that enables presenters to read a stream of text. So, in theory, you don't have to memorise anything. However, using a teleprompter is a skill in itself. There's a reason TV news anchors are paid so much.

TOP TIPS: THE TELEPROMPTER

Read your script out loud, in advance

Just because you'll be reading your script from the screen, it doesn't mean you can avoid practising it out loud ahead of time. The more familiar you are with your script in terms of how it's spoken out loud, the more natural you will be when you're delivering it. You will have already identified what needs to change, whether that was punctuation, emphasis on certain words or lengthy paragraphs that needed to be cut down into smaller sentences.

Set your own speed

If your event has a teleprompter, it will have a teleprompter operator too – a real human who is there to help you get the best from the machine. If you feel that the script on the screen is going too slow or too fast for you, the operator can help adjust the speed of the words so that it meets the pace of your delivery. And they can also adjust text size too. So there's no need to be squinting in an attempt to read a series of tiny words – which is never a good look.

Be aware of your body language

When using a teleprompter, it can be tempting to stand in front of a lectern and focus purely on reading your script without giving any thought to your body language. Gestures with your hands, facial expressions and purposeful movement add energy to your presentation. Think about (and practise) the areas in your presentation that would benefit from gesture, pausing, a step away from the lectern or a step to the side – anything that changes the tempo without being a distraction.

AT WORK – ZOOM, TEAMS, GOOGLE MEET ET AL.

With hybrid working now the norm, all of us are giving more and more presentations online. And we have probably all been on the receiving end of some really terrible, overly long, overly charted, boring presentations as a result. For the audience, the upside of Zoom, Teams and other video conferencing software is that we can turn off our video, put ourselves on mute and have the presentation rolling in the background. The downside is that, if we are the one giving the presentation, we have completely lost our audience and wasted a lot of time and energy for zero impact. For all our sakes, given how many presentations we either give or receive every week at work, we owe it to ourselves to do better – both as presenters and as an audience member.

TOP TIPS: ZOOM /TEAMS/ GOOGLE

Take it seriously

It's not 'just' an online presentation. Treat it as you would do a presentation or speech that you are making to a 'live' audience, in real life. Plan and prepare the same way – be clear on who your audience is, establish a clear structure (beginning, middle, end) and practise it plenty of times so you feel comfortable with the delivery. Being on camera requires even more ruthless editing – because there's so little body language for you to use in order to emphasise your points.

Set up for success

Don't rely on the in-built microphone in your laptop. Make sure you test the sound quality in advance and, if it's not good enough, buy an additional quality microphone or headset to ensure your voice is heard clearly – and that you can also hear clearly. Be intentional about the room you use – is it well-lit? Can you position your camera at eye level, so the audience isn't looking up your nose or down on top of your head? Avoid any backlighting that could obscure your face or make you 'bleach out'. People are much more forgiving about the blend of the personal with the professional since Covid, so it's not always necessary to add a fake or blurred background when you're presenting. But, as always, it depends on the audience and the image you wish to portray. You in your home office with a backdrop of bookcases is one thing; you in the spare room with a rack full of laundry in the background is another. Backdrops can be a distraction and you want your audience to be listening to you, not trying to read the poster in your bedroom. In the same vein, minimise distractions by:

- silencing your phone
- asking someone to take the dog for a walk so it doesn't bark (not everyone finds your dog's ear-splitting bark endearing)
- if you have one of those doorbells that offers a choice of twenty-four ringtones, make sure your children haven't set it up to crow like a rooster. That way, you'll avoid jumping out of your skin when the Amazon delivery guy arrives and having to explain to your audience why it sounds like a barnyard in your home office ... The point is to *think* about the image you want to convey and make sure you're well-lit, easy to hear, comfortable and you leave no hostages to fortune that will interrupt the meeting or distract you and your audience.

Have a back-up plan

The internet drops out, your presentation won't load, you can't manage the chat function and read your script at the same time – PANIC! Murphy's Law says: anything that can go wrong will go wrong. Your job is to try and anticipate all that can possibly go wrong and allow for it.

If you are involving your audience in polls or chat or breakout rooms, ask someone to join you to manage those elements so you can focus on facilitating the meeting and the content of your presentation. It's really hard to be a manager and play on the pitch so give yourself a break. Give your helper the presentation too so if your connection goes down, they can get the slides up quickly. If possible, have your phone ready with a hotspot connection in case you need it. If appropriate (i.e., you know exactly who will be attending and you have their email addresses), you can share your presentation with the audience in advance so they can follow along should there be any technical issues.

Get familiar with the features

You've probably done hundreds if not thousands of Zoom-type meetings since the dark days of Covid-19 lockdown. By now you probably feel that you know each platform pretty well. But with new features regularly being added to each, it's worth spending some time familiarising yourself with what's on offer beyond screen sharing, chat and participant management. Interactive whiteboards, polls and screen-sharing in breakout rooms are all features that can involve your audience and therefore make your time together more engaging and productive. It's also a good idea to have a basic understanding of troubleshooting techniques in case technical issues arise. And, for those who couldn't attend or for your own reference, consider recording your presentation. Remember that you'll need to ask permission from the audience to do this if you are planning to include any of them in the recording.

Get on early

When things go wrong, it feels like time suddenly accelerates to warp speed with the result that the 10 minutes you allowed yourself to turn up and get settled in advance suddenly feels like you're in the last 30 seconds of defusing an unexploded bomb trying to get your presentation to load before the start time. Give yourself the luxury of getting online 30 minutes before your scheduled delivery time. If you get set up and sorted with 25 minutes to go, no matter. Enjoy that cup of coffee while you wait for everyone to arrive. But if things do go wrong (the presentation won't load, no one can hear you, the camera isn't working), you've got a time buffer to sort it out. Plus, it's helpful for you and your audience if they log on and there's you – smiling, relaxed, welcoming – ready to go and clearly in control.

Create your own teleprompter

If you're giving a PowerPoint presentation, write a script for each slide. This ensures you don't waffle on but clearly and concisely deliver the key points instead. If you have the luxury of a desktop computer and a laptop, you can run the presentation on your Zoom/Teams call on your laptop and have the notes page open on your PC. Set up the two screens so it looks like you are looking directly at the audience and read your script with your peripheral vision. As with the teleprompter top tips, you should have practised in advance so you know what's coming up, where to put emphasis, etc. This will enable you to make eye contact with your on-screen audience as you go.

If you don't have two screens, you can still script your presentation. Print out the script slide by slide and make sure you have numbered each page to the relevant slide so you don't lose your way. Place your script in front of you attached to a clipboard so it is at eye level. You'll have to practise gently pulling each page away so you can fluidly move onto the next slide but putting the script in front of you, as if you were reading from a screen, will ensure you keep your eye contact level with your audience, rather than having your head down reading from papers on your desk. If you prefer to have your notes or script lying flat on your desk, make sure you're familiar enough with the content to confine yourself to the odd glance down. Asking your audience questions or checking in with them to ensure that they are following provides time for you to glance down and focus on your next chart or point.

Keep the slides simple

As with every presentation, think about what you really need to include on the slide itself. As a rule – more visuals, fewer words. If you need to show data, keep it to one key chart per slide. You want the content to be concise and focused to avoid overwhelming your audience with too much information. No doubt there will be some scientific research in the future that explains why sitting in front of a screen listening to someone else speak is exhausting, but for now, we know simply from our own experience that this is the case. Be kind to your audience and make it easy for them to listen and follow along. You can do this by avoiding overcrowding your slides and reducing their number.

Encourage participation

Ask people to keep their cameras on as you speak. They may not all do it, but they are more likely to do so if you ask. Ideally, you want to avoid speaking into the dark void created by a screen of tiny black rectangles. You can also encourage participation through polls, use interactive whiteboard apps, put people into breakout rooms and ask questions to keep them focused.

Sit up

Next time you have a Teams-type meeting, practise sitting in the best possible position. Too often we don't think about where the camera is, how low or high our chair is or what space we are taking up. Be intentional about how you sit – think BBC: 'Bum Back in Chair'. Sit right back into your chair with both feet firmly on the ground. Look into the camera – is your body taking up the middle of the screen and is your head roughly in the middle of the screen? Try different positions until you find one that makes you look like you are taking up the right amount of space, filling the screen appropriately so that you are looking at your audience directly. Be front and centre.

Don't rush

In the same way you would think about delivery if you were on a stage, be intentional about it when you present in the virtual world. Speak clearly, use emphasis when you need to and avoid rushing through your content in a monotone. Even on Zoom or Teams, it's helpful to use gestures and facial expressions to convey your energy and enthusiasm. Don't fixate your eye contact on your slides alone but look into your camera and, if it helps, imagine you are speaking to one or two people in particular in the audience. If you engage with them, it's likely the rest of the audience will think you are looking at them given that the participant squares that all of us see on Zoom/Teams/Google will be in a different order on screen for each person.

Be ready to drop the slides

When you're sharing a screen and showing a presentation, your audience will be made up of small on-screen squares. The bigger the audience, the smaller the squares. When there's no presentation, the squares are bigger. So far, so obvious. As you go through your presentation, there may be times when you want to involve your audience or when someone asks a question. At these times, be ready to come off slide share. Beyond making it easier to see you and for you to see the audience, dropping the slides at times helps to keep engagement, it allows you to pick up non-verbal cues from the audience because you can actually see them, and it makes you more approachable and relatable as it creates more interaction. Let your slides be a guide rather than the lead. You are the lead.

AT WORK – LIVE IN THE ROOM

As of May 2023, 39 per cent of workers in Great Britain advised that they had worked from home at some point in the previous seven days, with 73 per cent of British workers saying they had travelled to work in the last week. At the height of the first wave of the Coronavirus pandemic, in April 2020, almost half of UK workers were working from home, and just 31 per cent of people were travelling to work.[2] For many of us, being 'back in the office' is the norm – at least for three or four days a week – and with it comes the reality of presenting to people in 'real life'.

TOP TIPS – LIVE IN THE ROOM

Rehearse

It's tempting, when you regularly give presentations to an audience of your peers, to not bother with rehearsals. Often we cite lack of time as the reason for this, or perhaps we don't feel the audience is as 'important' as a room full of strangers. Your peers know you, you know them, so there's no need to be so formal, and rehearsing an internal presentation feels a bit over the top, doesn't it? Well, maybe. But what if you earned a reputation for being an excellent presenter who was always well prepared, who didn't fumble their words, who could get their message across clearly and credibly? What would be the impact of that reputation on your career? Get into the habit of rehearsing your presentations and you will only get better and better. You'll get noticed more and asked to present at company events. You may find you enjoy it so much that you look for opportunities outside of work. So many opportunities can come your way if you just factor in some time to run through your presentation and be *prepared*. Time spent rehearsing will pay you back tenfold.

Control your environment

If you regularly give presentations 'live' in the room at work, you might not think that any thought needs to be given to where the

---

[2] *Working Location Trends in Great Britain 2020–2023*, published by D. Clark, 6 June 2023.

presentation will take place. But you still need to give it some thought and control your environment so it suits *you* best. I've seen people give presentations where they're almost hiding behind a flipchart, or where a chair is in the way and they keep bumping into it or where they keep stepping on a squeaky floorboard, oblivious to the distracting noise.

It's amazing what you become oblivious to when you are presenting – especially if you are unrehearsed and have to focus entirely on thinking of the next word that has to come out of your mouth instead of being conscious of where you are or your environment and audience.

Be healthily paranoid – be that control freak. Check out the room in advance. Get the feel of it, the dimensions, the space where you can make most eye contact with the most people. Do this especially if you are presenting in a hybrid format: mixing offline with online. Hybrid meetings need extra thought and preparation because you'll need to make sure both your audience in the room *and* those participating from other locations can see you, hear you and join in. For example, make sure you sit close to the screen or camera and microphone linking you to the online participants – as lead presenter, you need to be the most visible and audible person in the room. Plus, you'll need to project your voice, and ask any participants who want to make a verbal contribution to do so too.

HOW WILL I PRESENT IT?

Omne trium perfectum
(Everything that comes in threes is perfect)

You're reading this book because you want shortcuts that can help improve both your presenting style and the presentation itself. When it comes to structuring your presentation, there is no better technique to use than the 'rule of three'.

According to science, three is the fewest number of elements required to create a pattern, and research also shows that our short-term memory recall is limited to three, maximum four items. That's why you see so many advertising slogans, political speeches, stories and book titles evoke words and phrases in threes. For example, we're all familiar with the phrase, 'blood, sweat and tears' which had its origins in a speech given by Winston Churchill to the House of Commons of the Parliament of the United Kingdom on 13 May 1940:

> We are in the preliminary stage of one of the greatest battles in history ... That we are in action at many points – in Norway and in Holland – that we have to be prepared in the Mediterranean. That the air battle is continuous, and that many preparations have to be made here at home.
>
> I would say to the House as I said to those who have joined this government: 'I have nothing to offer but blood, toil, tears and sweat'. We have before us an ordeal of the most grievous kind. We have before us many, many long months of struggle and of suffering.

What's interesting about this is that the word 'toil' has been dropped in favour of a re-jig of the words which makes them flow better and be more memorable. Received wisdom is that if you want something to stick in someone's head, put it in a sequence of three. That's why we remember Tony Blair's election priorities: 'Education, Education, Education'. Why we can instantly recall Mars bar's decades old strapline, 'Work, rest and play'. And, going back to ancient times, Julius Caesar's famous Latin phrase, 'Veni, vidi, vici' – 'I came, I saw, I conquered.'

While you may consider having a pithy three-word phrase in

your presentation, what's more useful is to use the 'rule of three' when structuring your communication.

WHAT IS THE RULE OF THREE?

Plays – unless they are written by William Shakespeare – typically, have a three-act structure. Films, books, stories – all are divided into three parts – the beginning, middle and end. And, within a PowerPoint presentation, three bullet points drive home the message more effectively and are more memorable than two or four.

The rule of three is a powerful technique for presenting. Any ideas, thoughts, events, characters or sentences that are presented in threes are more effective and memorable.

If we take the analogy of the play being in three acts, it becomes much easier to structure your presentation:

ACT ONE

The metaphorical curtain is up. The spotlight is on you. You need to start strong. I beg of you, don't start your presentation with lots of rambling 'thank you, thank you, I'm so grateful to be here, thanks for the opportunity' type words before you – finally – get to the point. And I can't tell you how many presentations I've sat through where the introduction took 10 minutes to cover what the presentation was going to be about. Just get to the good stuff and ditch the waffling. I'll share some great ways to open your presentation with impact shortly.

ACT TWO

Here the plot/story/presentation develops further. The audience either gets more involved or, if you don't keep their attention, loses interest and drifts off. In plays and stories, this is where tension is often introduced – via a plot twist, a change in direction or the introduction of a new character. In a business presentation, this is the heart of your story. It's where you're making your case – how will you respond to a budget crisis, create a recruitment drive, change the customer experience programme? What can you do to pull a 'rabbit out of the hat' at this point – a moment of insight or magic in your presentation that will make the audience sit up and take notice?

ACT THREE

Now for the conclusion. In Shakespeare, conflicts are resolved, loose ends are tied up and the play either ends on a high with reconciliation and love or in sorrow, with untimely death and recriminations. Cheery! For your presentation, it's likely to be the place where you make your recommendations or issue a call to action. It may well be the bulk of your presentation. How will you leave your audience feeling? Do you want them to feel confident, unsettled, reassured, ready to act? Hone into that feeling – it will help you come to a conclusion with clarity. You want to end on a bold and resolute note.

Taking each of these acts in turn, here's some practical examples of how you can ensure a strong beginning, middle and end.

ACT ONE: START STRONG

The internet is littered with 'clickbait' – headlines designed to entice you further and further down the rabbit hole of information you might find useful but probably won't. Whether it's 'The five things you MUST do to get promoted' or, more likely, 'People can't get enough of these pictures of *really hot* firefighters', the power of a strong headline as an attention grabber can't be denied.

The headline is designed to give you the gist of the story that follows and is a device that can be used in business to tighten up and improve communication. Whether it's the opening of a meeting, presentation, pitch, speech or the start of an online meeting, thinking of (and practising) your opening headline or sentence in advance will serve you well. It forces you to focus on the purpose driving what you want to say and ensures you start strong. So many people claim, 'I'm okay once I get going.' But, as an audience, do we really want to see and hear someone warming up in front of us? Plays, TV episodes, soap operas – would we pay good money to wait for the actors to struggle through the first few minutes before they hit their stride? Don't we prefer someone who starts with impact and keeps us engaged?

Be that presenter.

HOW TO DO IT

When I coach individuals and teams on improving the impact of their communications, there is one simple technique that people find really useful. It's the ABCD of opening your presentation:

Attention

What can you say that would be a creative way to capture your audience from the outset and make them want to listen to you? It could be a question, priming our curiosity and asking something we can relate to, empathise with or would like to see answered. Or it could be a challenging statement, a surprising fact or statistic. Whatever it is, it should be one crisp sentence before you move on to…

Benefits

Audiences are selfish – they want to know 'What's in it for me?' Your job here is to outline what they will gain from listening to you. What will they learn that they didn't know? What will they do differently as a result of hearing from you?

Credentials

Who are you and what gives you the right to speak on this subject?

You could also include a line about your company here. We call this the 'floating C' because in some instances – if you know the audience well, for example – you wouldn't need to include your credentials. In other situations, it may be better for you to introduce yourself ahead of your attention-grabbing opening remark.

Directions

Here's where you verbally outline the journey you'll take with your presentation, conference call or workshop. The audience feels reassured that they know where they are going and what you will cover.

The trick with the ABCD device is to *keep it tight*. It's not about creating a dense paragraph to cover each section, it's about one or two sentences per letter. Less is more. For example:

Attention: A recent survey revealed that the biggest fear in life is presenting in public. In second place, death.

Benefit: If you would rather die than give a presentation, I'm here to help save your life.

Credentials: I've been helping high-performing individuals and teams improve their communication impact for over twenty years, working with some of the world's most dynamic companies.

Direction: Over the next fifteen minutes I'm going to share the five tips to help take the fear out of facing an audience and then you can try the techniques out for yourself.

Easy to remember and straightforward to put into practice, give it a go the next time you're struggling to think how to start a meeting or presentation.

ACT ONE: TOP TIPS

Here are ten ideas to open your presentation with impact. A word of caution though. Your goal is to work out what is going to help you connect with your audience and not just come up with something that you think is really clever. So make it *relevant* and ensure it reflects your key points.

1. Ask a question. But make it a bold or provocative one. Make sure you're going to get the answer you want (for this you may need a 'plant' in the audience – someone who you've primed to shout out the answer) or quickly answer it yourself. Either way, ensure you pause for at least five seconds to let it land and give people a chance to respond:

a.   Do you remember when ... ?

b.   How many of you agree with this statement ... ?

c.   When was the last time you ... ?

d.   Where were you when ... ?

e.   Who, here, would describe themselves as an extrovert?

2. Tell a short story. An illustration of the challenge, the problem, the opportunity and the situation. Or a story about yourself (keep it brief!). What did it take to get to where you are today? What did you learn and why is it important? Here's how I opened a recent speech about networking and selling:

> *My first job began with crushing disappointment when I realised that the sound of the phone ringing was not my cue to lean back in my chair, put my feet up on the desk and remove my massive clip-on earring before putting the receiver to my ear. I would not be settling into intense conversations uttering, 'Yes?' and, 'Uh-huh' and, 'Be right*

there' before slamming the phone down, dashing out the door and hailing a cab that would immediately screech to a halt at my feet. Turns out I was not kick-ass Drew Barrymore in the reboot of Charlie's Angels. *Instead, I was a junior account executive at an agency in Bermondsey, South London, and my biggest client was a shopping centre crèche called the Hippo Club. Glamour was low. The phone was silent.*

But one thing my job did involve was an introduction to trade shows and what they're all about – namely networking and selling.

3. Imagine if . . . paint the picture of the future in words: what will success look like? How will your idea work? Help the audience see it, feel it, even taste it.

Imagine we're sitting here, one year from now. Our company has grown from twenty-nine people to two hundred. Our profit margins are a healthy 20 per cent and our pipeline is full of quality leads for interesting projects. We've just won the 'company of the year' award and celebrated by taking the whole company for an off-site strategy meeting in the South of France. Sounds too good to be true? I'm here to make the case that not only is this possible, it's probably not ambitious enough. Let me explain why . . .

You'd have to listen, wouldn't you? You'd *want* to listen.

4. Use an analogy. What can you share from history, nature, entertainment or sport? I don't care if this example dates me because some legends will always be part of the zeitgeist, even if they were born over a hundred years ago. Here's how I opened a speech called, 'The Frank Sinatra Guide to Pitching'.

> *Francis Albert Sinatra: musician, actor, lover, legend and a personal idol of mine since I first saw him in the film* On the Town *when I was eight. Whether on stage or off, Sinatra's mantra was 'all or nothing at all' – either give it 100 per cent or don't even bother. It's a mantra I believe true not just for life but for pitching too. For, as he said, 'You can be the most artistically perfect performer in the world, but an audience is like a broad – if you're indifferent, Endsville.'*
>
> *So, as a rallying cry for the end of indifferent, half-hearted pitches and in tribute to the one and only Chairman of the Board, here's my, What would Frank do? Guide to the Golden Rules of Pitching.*

5. Use a prop. If you've watched the film *The Big Short* which chronicles the actions of several finance industry professionals in the mid-2000s, you'll remember the scene where Ryan Gosling's character foreshadows the dramatic collapse of the USA real estate market using the wooden block game Jenga. Each block represented a mortgage bond which, when removed, rapidly caused the whole tower to fall. It was a short, memorable and dramatic way of illustrating his point.

When I'm coaching clients about the importance of eye contact with the audience, I often bring a handful of sweets with me. If I throw all the sweets up into the air, the audience doesn't know where to focus and won't see where all the sweets land. But if I throw the sweets one by one at different people in the audience, I know they will catch the sweet – but only if I have eye contact with them. It's a visual metaphor to make the point about the importance of eye contact. Eye contact makes a connection with the audience and ensures your message (the sweets) is both caught and retained.

What prop could you use that would capture the audience's attention and help you make your point?

6. Start with the challenge. 'Since January we have fallen behind on our projected revenue by 5 per cent month on month. If this carries on at the same rate to the end of the year, we will be behind target by $X million. Here's my plan on how to get back on track in the next three months.'

7. Start with the opportunity. Same approach, different angle. 'It will take six months and six new clients to make our numbers by the end of the year. This is my plan for how to do it.'

8. Play a video. It could be a clip from YouTube, it could be a vox pop interview from the target consumer. Or it could be a short and snappy montage set to music to set the mood for the rest of your presentation. There's inspiration and so many great ideas on TikTok and Instagram, and if you don't know how to create your own, ask the nearest millennial or Gen Z-er!

9. Start with a quote. This can stray into 'motivational quotes on the internet' territory but, if delivered well and relevant to your content, can still be a bold and compelling way of opening with impact. Reading a short passage from a book can also set the scene.

Five examples:
A rallying cry: 'I am desperate for change – now – not in eight years or twelve years but right now.'
MICHELLE OBAMA

The size of the task: 'Let the blood and the bruises define your legacy.'
LADY GAGA

Time to speak up: 'There is a time for silence. There is a time for waiting your turn. But if you know how you feel and you so clearly know what you need to say, you'll know it. I don't think you should wait. I think you should speak now.'
TAYLOR SWIFT

Vulnerability: 'I reserve the right to be a mess and completely unlikable.'
VIOLA DAVIS

The case for action: 'Gentleness doesn't get work done unless you happen to be a hen laying eggs.'
COCO CHANEL

Even if you decide not to use a quote in the end, often I find that doing a Google search on 'quotes about motivation' or 'quotes about the need for change' (or whatever your subject is) can give me some ideas for openings or language or themes to use. And if nothing quite fits what you want to say then start with a quote from yourself!

10. Tell a joke. Only if your name is Amy Schumer.

ACT TWO: AVOIDING THE SNOOZE ZONE

This is the meat of your presentation and the place where you make your case. It's also the danger zone for your audience as, if you're not careful, they can get lost in a sea of words before drifting off, their attention lost forever. To ensure the second act of your presentation keeps your audience's attention, think 'less is more'.

One of the 'warm-up' exercises I often do in workshops is to put people into pairs and ask one person to tell the other person their life story, from birth until the present day. The catch is, they only have one minute to do it. Initially, it feels like such a limited amount of time to cover a lot of ground but, once they get going, they realise that they can pack a lot of information into a small amount of time. Most people follow chronological order, talking through the key milestones of where they were born, where they went to school and the journey they took to get to where they are working today. Very occasionally, someone will jump into the middle of their life story and focus on a particular aspect of their life – perhaps they lived in a number of different countries, or there was a moment in their life which took them in a different direction. There's no right or wrong way to approach this exercise. It's designed to get people talking, sharing something of themselves, and to show that you can cover a lot of ground in one minute.

Which is telling, because when it comes to speeches and presentations, there is still a tendency to err on the lengthy side. Business presentations and pitches are often scheduled for 30 minutes to 45 minutes, sometimes even an hour. That's a lot of content – a big second act – and a big ask to keep your audience engaged.

If you do have to fill this amount of time, you are going to have to work to keep the audience's attention. You'll need to change things up. Here are three ways to 'change gear' in the middle of your presentation.

ACT TWO: TOP TIPS
1. Involve the audience

Yes, the dreaded words 'audience participation'. It's not without risk as some audiences don't want to participate; they want to be passive recipients of your message. So if you ask them to get involved, you may be met with a blank wall of non-cooperation. Rather than asking a random question in the hope of getting a response, you may need to think of a different route. One successful example of this I witnessed was a speaker who had stuck an envelope under the seat of every chair in the room. Halfway through her presentation, she asked the audience to find and open their envelope. One of the envelopes gave the finder a prize. The act of everyone scrabbling under their chairs and opening their envelopes changed the energy in the room, which the presenter then built on when she got back to her speech.

2. Change the media

You don't always have to be the one talking all the time. You can bring in a video clip or play a short piece of music to illustrate your point. Your goal in this middle section is to make the audience sit up and pay attention by employing their other senses.

3. Bring on a special guest

Beloved of performers worldwide, the crowd goes wild when an unexpected guest arrives on stage to join the lead singer in a duet. What is your equivalent of Harry Styles bringing on Taylor Swift? It may not result in a roar from the audience but if you're giving a presentation about the customer experience, bringing on a customer (prepared, rehearsed) to share their point of view is more impactful than a slide with a quote written on it. Similarly, bringing in a colleague from the business that you haven't announced in advance and doing a 'double-header' presentation midway through keeps it lively and engaging.

If you can avoid committing to a lengthy presentation, you should always try to do so. An example we should all try to emulate is TED talks.

TED is dedicated to researching and sharing knowledge that matters through short talks and presentations. Its goal is to inform and educate global audiences in an accessible way. Scientists, researchers, technologists, business leaders, artists, designers and other world experts take the TED stage to present 'Ideas Worth Spreading': interesting and engaging talks on their subject matter. Crucially, each TED talk lasts no longer than 18 minutes. We can all learn from the TED approach, which is to take complex ideas and communicate them in an accessible and memorable way. At the end of this chapter, I share an approach that is not the official TED presentation structure but is a useful way of mapping out your presentation or speech so you cover everything you need to within the 18-minute deadline.

But before that, let's look at how to finish your presentation so that you end as strongly as you started.

ACT THREE: END ON A HIGH

Make the conclusion as powerful as you can. In musical theatre, the best song is saved until last so the audience leaves still humming the tune. Same for you. You don't need to burst into a rousing chorus of 'Let It Go' but you should pay attention to your final conclusion/ remark. What the audience hears last is what they will take away, so conclude with power.

ACT THREE: TOP TIPS
1. Link the ending to the beginning.

Many books, films and magazine articles bring the ending round to the beginning. What I mean by that is that they come back to a story or an image that they referenced at the start and conclude the 'show' by making sense of it. Examples of this would be the diner scene in *Pulp Fiction* that opens the film. As the audience, we don't understand what's going on until the end of the film when we're back in the diner and the pieces of the story finally add up. Or it may be a visual cue, as in the film *The Wizard of Oz*, one of the first colour films back in the 1930s. It started in black and white, transformed to colour when Dorothy entered the world of Oz and returns to black and white film when Dorothy gets back to Kansas. If you can link your ending to the beginning, it's a neat device that has the audience thinking 'ooh – that's clever!'

2. Have a call to arms

What's the rallying cry that you want to end with? You've probably covered what you want the audience to think and feel; what do you want them to *do*? Make it clear.

3. Get your body and voice behind your message

Too many presentations end not with a bang but with a whimper. They trail off with a lame . . . 'er, that's it, thanks'. Whatever you decide to end with, make sure that you deliver your message with clarity and boldness. Take a pause. Look the audience in the eye. Say your final line. Pause again. Say thank you. Then pause again for – we hope – the rapturous applause. Don't run off the stage in huge relief that the dreaded experience is over. Take the applause – you've earned it.

Putting it all together, here's a structure to help you create an eighteen-minute speech. Add in any of the ideas we've just covered to bring the content to life.

EIGHTEEN-MINUTE SPEECH IN FIVE STEPS

Topic: What's the title of your speech?
Purpose: What's the effect you want to have on your audience? How do you want them to think and feel? And what do you want them to *DO*?
Bullet point your message for each step:

ONE: Attention – make them sit up and listen. A bold opening remark/ABCD opening (1 minute)

TWO: What's in it for them? What benefit will the audience get from listening to you? Expand on the benefit if you've mentioned this in your ABCD opener (2 minutes)

THREE: Main point. What do you want to change or get them to do? And why should they change and do as you suggest? (6 minutes)

FOUR: Examples – a maximum of three points/illustrations/stories to make your case (7 minutes)

Within steps three and four – add an 'Act Two' idea to change gear and keep the audience engaged)

FIVE: Call to action. A snappy summary, a link back to the start, a call to arms (2 minutes)

PRESENTING AS A TEAM

What happens when it's not just you in the spotlight but one or more of your colleagues too? It could be a project you've been working on with others or a pitch to a prospective client. Suddenly it's not just your personal presentation you have to worry about, it's other people's as well. Don't panic.

Essentially, the same planning elements from this chapter apply as for a solo presentation in terms of who, why, where and what. You have to plan. But above all, you have to rehearse. Together. Getting people to commit to rehearsing together is often the hardest part. But it's vital to have run through your presentation together at least three times ahead of the real thing.

Why three times? Well, the first rehearsal, as we all know, isn't really a rehearsal; it's a walk through the deck of charts where you take out some, rewrite others and move the rest around. No one actually rehearses! If you get to a second run through, everyone knows their bit, but the thing probably doesn't hold together as a whole yet. It's only on the third rehearsal that the magic happens. When each presenter is familiar not just with their bit but with the content of the other presenters and, crucially, when each cue for a handover or comment from someone else on the team gets practised.

As a team you'll need to agree:

Roles: Who is physically controlling the presentation? Or, if you are presenting offline, are you handing the slide clicker between you like a baton as each new presenter begins their piece?

Who is opening the presentation? What's the speaking order? Would it work if the person who opened the presentation also closes it? Or should you all just take turns in speaking? Will there be any interplay between you so you present together, batting the presentation to and fro as a sort of double (or triple, or however many) act?

All these details need to be thought about and practised in advance to aid a smooth flow.

Staging: Are you sitting or standing? Or a mixture of both? A rehearsal will reveal whether you look like a seamless team gracefully standing up at specific times to make a point or a group of disparate people popping up and down at random moments with no chemistry between you and no narrative flow to your presentation.

Handovers: My personal pet hate in team presentations is when someone finishes their part by saying, 'I'm now going to hand over to Peggy who's going to talk through this quarter's figures'. And then Peggy starts her part of the presentation by saying, 'Thanks, Nancy. I'm now going to talk through this quarter's figures.' Argh! It sounds so clunky. That approach works if you are on a regional news channel, but not in a pitch or presentation. Rehearsing as a team means you know when each other's part comes to an end and you can seamlessly start your part of the presentation without the need for a clunky handover. Doing this well makes you look like a slick team that works seamlessly together.

Q&A: Even a polished presentation can fall down in the question-and-answer session as often it's the part the team hasn't rehearsed, due to lack of time or lack of thought. Treat the Q&A as an extension of the presentation or pitch. Think about all the questions you would ask if you saw your presentation for the first time. Think about the questions you'd hate to be asked on the day – because the audience probably will ask them. Then agree as a team who will answer questions by key themes and how you will answer all the questions you've just anticipated in a succinct way. Then practise doing it.

There may be varying levels of confidence and presenting skill in a team pitch or presentation but as long as you come across as a team – supportive of each other, at ease and playing to each other's strengths – your audience will recognise that and respond positively to you all.

PLANNING – A CAUTIONARY TALE

We were pitching to handle the pan-European announcement of a merger between two global research companies. Best practice would have the presentation completed and rehearsed 24 hours ahead of the pitch. Reality had us in the office at 3 a.m. on what we considered to be Friday evening but was in fact Saturday morning, still making changes to the PowerPoint with no one daring to mention the word rehearsal.

Due to the clients flying in from various locations, the pitch was being held at a hotel near Heathrow airport on the same Saturday morning that we were still in the office. Finally finishing at 5 a.m., we took two hours to go home and change before meeting in the hotel lobby. Jacked up on double espressos, we (the MD and me, a lowly account manager at the time) stared wide-eyed at each other. The door opened: we were on.

It was the olden days, so we had to bring our own projector and laptop. We duly set it all up and turned it on. Nothing. Tried again. Nothing. We were one of four agencies presenting; there was a strict timetable. We didn't have time for this. No matter – we were prepared! We had bound documents of the presentation – we could talk through those.

I handed them out to the client prospects. Immediately, they did what all clients do when faced with an agency document. They turned to the last page to look at the budget. Whereupon my boss yelled 'Don't look at that!' at the client and snatched the document from his hand, before turning the book back to the beginning and starting our pitch.

Troopers that we were, we ploughed through the pitch, then shuffled out of the room under the gaze of the other three agencies lining up for their turn. I went home and slept for 24 hours. What a waste of time and effort.

On Monday, I came into the office and was told we had won the pitch. WTF! Why?! How?!

Because it turned out that one of the clients (the one who had flicked to the back of the book) was known to be 'tricky' and the other party in the merger wanted an agency who would not be afraid to stand up to him. As was clearly demonstrated in our pitch.

The moral of that story is that sometimes, despite your worst efforts, luck shines on you. That said, better to rely on planning and preparation rather than luck if you really want to get ahead.

3.
Reason

'The success of your presentation will be judged not by the
knowledge you send but by what the listener receives.'
LILLY WALTERS

People don't just buy *what* brands do, they also buy into *why* they do
things in a particular way. Having a higher purpose casts a brand's
offer in a more appealing light and acts as a beacon to attract
customers whose values align with their own. Apple's purpose is 'to
make the best products on earth and to leave the world better than
we found it'. For Patagonia: 'We're in business to save our home
planet – to build the best product, cause no unnecessary harm, use
business to protect nature, and not be bound by convention.' Lest we
forget, Apple is the largest company on the planet by market
capitalisation and Patagonia's commitment to saving the planet has
been instrumental to its success for decades.

The best presentations are also incredibly clear on what their
purpose – or reason – is for existing. But, what's different for
presentations is that you can have an overall purpose and then
different 'moment-to-moment' purposes throughout the presentation.
Unlike Apple or Patagonia, who pride themselves on being
intentionally consistent, we go through a whole gamut of reasons
when we communicate.

Let's use the analogy of a hat.

What's the reason for wearing a hat?

To keep your head dry when it rains? Well, yes, but you can also
wear a hat to stop the sun from burning your scalp. So the overall

reason for a hat is to protect.

But a hat can exist for many other reasons too.

- Stick a logo on it and its reason for being is to advertise.
- Add some bells and its reason is to be festive.
- In the hands of a milliner such as Stephen Jones or Philip Treacy, it becomes a work of art with the ability to inspire or shock.
- Take a hat off, turn it upside down and it becomes a vessel to carry things in.

You get the picture. There are multiple reasons for a hat's use.

In a presentation, our overall reason for doing it can be to convince, to perform, to persuade, to sell or to inform. All well and good but it's hard for our body and our voice to know what to do in order to 'sell'. But if I want to *excite* you about a product, it is much easier for me to instinctively know how to deliver that emotion.

As well as being clear on what the reason for your presentation is, you need to be clear on what you want your audience to think, feel or do as a result of listening to you.

Once you have established that, it becomes much easier to use your body and voice to 'change gear' throughout the presentation and thus avoid the monotonous monologues that we all dread to hear.

Here are some readymade reasons and motivations to help you think about what you want people to think, feel and do throughout your presentation. Note that 'bore' is included. It's unlikely to be a reason you want to communicate to your audience but it's one that can occur if you are not intentional about providing an alternative!

| Annoy | Challenge | Hearten | Reward | Welcome |
| Advise | Praise | Punish | Nag | Quiz |

Beg	Bore	Relax	Lecture	Sadden
Reassure	Scare	Gratify	Melt	Shame
Tempt	Enthral	Hush	Quieten	Shock
Cajole	Amaze	Irritate	Puzzle	Tease
Impress	Move	Tantalise	Thrill	Discourage
Pressurise	Rouse	Urge	Inspire	Coax
Provoke	Torment	Startle	Patronise	Deflate
Mock	Muddle	Support	Threaten	Fire up
Motivate	Unsettle	Intimidate	Warn	Dominate
Revive	Vindicate	Scrutinise		

BRINGING IT TO LIFE

Another exercise that helps your body and voice get behind your words to deliver your message is to imagine you are someone else. Now, I'm not suggesting we move into the potentially uncomfortable territory of amateur dramatics, but it can be helpful to imagine different roles or characters for the different elements of your presentation.

This is an approach that global superstar singer Beyoncé revealed when she released her album, *I Am... Sasha Fierce*. She explained that Sasha Fierce was her on-stage persona – her more confident alter-ego. Describing her, Beyoncé said, 'Sasha Fierce is the fun, more sensual, more aggressive, more outspoken side and more glamorous side that comes out when I am working and when I am on the stage.'

If it's good enough for Beyoncé, it's good enough for us. We won't necessarily need to become Sasha Fierce, but we can certainly channel some of her confidence. If you had an alter ego, what would they be called? What attributes would they have? Would they worry about what people think of them? (No.) Would they look forward to giving their presentation? (Yes.) Try it until eventually you won't need to imagine you are someone else. After all, Beyoncé no longer goes by her alter ego Sasha Fierce.

Maybe even create a character or persona for each part of your presentation.

If you want to open your presentation with a warm welcome, think of who you consider to be the most appealing, friendly and engaging TV host – is that Davina McCall, Stephen Colbert or Ant and Dec? Imagine you are one of them as you walk onto the stage – how would you behave? You'd probably have a big smile on your face, you might give a wave to the audience, you'd definitely walk on with energy and enthusiasm.

Or perhaps you have to give some sobering news to your audience. Imagine you are a police inspector outside New Scotland Yard giving a press conference. What would your body language be like then? You'd have to deliver the news more slowly to enable the media to hear the key messages. You'd probably have to summarise your statement at the end. The tone would be serious and you would want to convey that you are on top of the situation so your audience feels reassured.

If your purpose is to excite your audience, maybe you imagine you are a primary school teacher and your audience is an enthusiastic group of children who respond positively to your energy. You don't need to be patronising and fake; you do need to be passionate about your subject and willing to share that enthusiasm knowing that children can spot a phoney a mile off.

Whatever the 'moment to moment' reason is throughout your presentation, it can be helpful to imagine how you would present that section if you were to take on a particular character. And, if you still really hate the idea of presenting at all, imagining you are someone completely different – your confident alter ego who loves the limelight – can help get rid of some of that negative self-talk that gets in the way of us doing a great job. Eventually, you'll find that you don't need an alter-ego or to play a character – the essential you is perfectly good enough.

REASON – A CAUTIONARY TALE

I'm still haunted by a pitch I was involved in for a well-known car tyre manufacturer. The company I worked for at the time had a team of ten working on this pitch... But as a team we hadn't met in person – all our communication had been done via conference calls and email.

Our overall reason or purpose for the pitch presentation was to show the clients that we were a seamless global team that could work in total harmony with their seamless global team. We knew that it was important to show strength and depth across our network and to demonstrate that we regularly worked together on cross-border assignments. The reality was that we didn't have many truly global campaigns at that time and none of us had previously worked together except for in the two weeks prior to this pitch. Never mind. We knew that in theory we could work together and surely that was enough? Fake it until you make it and all that...

On the day of the pitch, the London team was late due to delays on the Eurostar. This meant there was no time for a full rehearsal – or even a short one. We entered what, in my memory, was the biggest boardroom I have ever seen and scattered ourselves around the table. An equally large contingent sat opposite us on the client side.

Our pitch leader waxed lyrical about our team. This was no ordinary team. This was a truly global team – a seamless group of experts who regularly worked together on multi-market programmes. This was, 'a network that *works*'.

'And now,' he said, 'to explain that further, I'd like to hand over to Sandrine from the Paris office.'

'I'm Claudette,' said 'Sandrine'.

Perhaps that wasn't the only reason we lost that pitch, but it felt like it at the time.

4.
Impact

'*You don't have to be the voice of a generation, but you can be an important voice in the conversation.*'
ANONYMOUS

Anyone who drives a car in the UK or Europe will be familiar with signs like this one. These 30 mph or kmph road signs are placed at regular intervals in built up areas. Is it clear what they are saying to the driver? Absolutely. Are there adequate opportunities for drivers to see them? Absolutely.

Yet – ask any speed-awareness course facilitator – far too few drivers ever react to these signs. Because, in spite of the clarity of the

message, in spite of all the opportunities to see the message, these signs are designed from the point of view of what is *put into* the communication, not what is *taken out of it*. They are the road-side equivalent of wallpaper we fail to notice and, most importantly, when viewed in isolation, they carry no cost or consequence for non-compliance . . . or any reward for compliance.

Most corporate communication, emails, presentations, proposals and speeches are written in the same way as a 30 mph road sign. They focus on the sender's input rather than the audience's *take out*. With exactly the same result. Nothing changes, no one actually *does* anything new or different. What a waste of time and effort to create a presentation that causes no change.

Now, consider the bright yellow speed camera, looming towards you. Does a speed camera have an effect on driver behaviour? You bet it does. Why? Because it carries a sanction – there are immediate implications for ignoring its presence. It communicates from the point of view of the message the driver *takes out*, not from the point of view of what is *put into* the communication.

This is a fundamentally different start point. One from which every piece of communication must start. Our communication must always drive action, impel urgency to act and do. It must show that there are *consequences* and warn of the dangers of inaction or maintaining the status quo. More positively, it must demonstrate the opportunities that are available if we do act. In contrast to speed cameras, there are also road signs that display smiley faces in reaction to drivers slowing down to the legal speed limit. We are simple creatures and this basic emotional reward for behaving well encourages compliance. The point is someone, somewhere, was thinking about the audience.

We need to do this too if we wish to have 'impact' when we speak. We only succeed if we inspire or compel our audience to act.

If you are going to the trouble of putting a presentation together, don't you want it to have impact? Otherwise, you're spending a lot of time and effort to make nothing happen.

Nowhere is this demonstrated more keenly than in the competitive pitch. Again and again, I see people in companies that are phenomenally good at their craft, produce demonstratively superior results for their clients, have cleverer people than their competitors, but who lose pitch after pitch to companies that are half as good as they are. Why? Because they keep giving deathly-dull presentations that fail to inspire or engage. Whereas these companies' inferior competitors know that they are unlikely to produce a better solution; instead, they focus on the 'soft stuff' – they get to understand the audience and what makes them tick. They fizz with effort and energy to show what a dynamic team they are. And they win the pitch because it's not just about the content. It's as much about *how* the content is presented.

So this is where we focus on putting on a fantastic show. Companies that are technically brilliant problem-solvers focus on the technicalities and solving the problem (big surprise). Their competitors, who aren't as technically proficient, focus on the show. It's like the difference between high street fashion retailers. Some fashion retailers have dazzling window displays – sexy, everchanging and exciting – designed to draw you in. But the merchandise is often shoddily made and doesn't last. Other retailers have dull, dreary and functional shop windows but their merchandise is robust, well-made and of excellent value. Trouble is, customers like the excitement of the sexy shop window. So they choose inferior goods because the *promise* of the experience is superior.

Dazzle your audience. Think how powerful you'd be if you had great merchandise *and* a sexy shop window. If you could put the sheen of showmanship on your palpably superior product then you'd win every pitch, get every client to buy your recommendation and win the hearts and minds of your employees and all those other important stakeholders. Wouldn't that be good? Okay. But how?

You might be thinking that 'dazzle' is code for time-consuming, expensive and over-the-top largesse. But did I say that I want you to create a spectacular show with dry ice, loads of special effects and dancers? No. (Well, not unless the brief calls for it.) Dazzle doesn't mean empty or expensive pazazz.

Let's take a step back and look at the impact on our communication in terms of our physicality. Newsflash: your PowerPoint slides, your visual aids, your clever props are not your presentation, YOU are your presentation. Here's why:

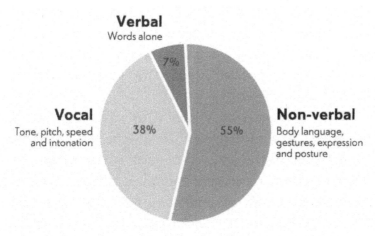

Sources: McHugo et al 1985; Lanone & Schrott 1989

You may have seen this chart before. It's quite well known and has been circulating in the business world since the 1960s. It comes from research published by the psychologist Professor Albert Mehrabian from the University of California, Los Angeles. However, it is often misunderstood. Mehrabian's experiments focused on how emotion is communicated. He tested reactions to dissonance between the words being spoken and the tone of voice and body language being used. For example, if someone says, 'I'm so angry' but says it softly and with a warm smile on their face, the words don't count for much. What Professor Mehrabian was trying to show is that the three elements – vocal, verbal and non-verbal – work together. When they do, that makes for the most effective communication. But this research is often misrepresented. People often think that because the words we use only contribute 7 per cent to our overall communication Mehrabian was saying words don't really matter at all. He was not saying that any words we say when we are communicating are effectively irrelevant. Nor was he saying that we should just focus on developing a presenting style that is all about body language and tone of voice.

What the professor was saying is that we need our body and our voice to 'back' our words – to reinforce them physically, orally and aurally. When they do, they endow so much more meaning to our articulated message. Essentially, it's what we say *and* how we say it that has the biggest impact.

This may seem obvious. After all, don't we all communicate like this every day in our conversations with family, friends and colleagues? Yes, we do (usually). The trick is to translate that completely natural way of communicating when we are presenting to an audience. For many people, the interplay between words, body and tone of voice can disappear under pressure. Under stress, all that remains is the words, bereft of the life our personal animation would normally give them. When this happens, it's a dead giveaway that we are feeling out of control and nervous.

BODY LANGUAGE AND TONE OF VOICE

From an audience point of view, the most visible 'tell' on how they perceive our level of confidence (and therefore, our credibility) is our body language. The way our physical behaviour, expression and mannerisms communicate to others – without us saying a word.

When we're speaking with friends and family our body language is often done instinctively – we're not consciously aware of the wordless signals we are giving out; and when we are in dialogue with others, we're also receiving similar wordless signals from others. By the time we reach adult age, we're pretty good at 'reading' body language. We can tell whether we are picking up signals that are approving, encouraging, bored or hostile, even if the words that person is saying seem to contradict this.

For example, have you ever had a situation with a partner or friend who you can clearly see, through their body language, is annoyed? Yet, when you ask what the matter is, they reply:

'NOTHING! I'm FINE!'

If you took their words at face value, you'd assume all is well. After all, that's what they told you. But their body language is telling a whole different story – they are radiating hostility and anger through their tense physicality, their angry face and their inability to keep eye contact. And their tone of voice – a bit too emphatic, a bit too cross – also gives the lie to the words being spoken.

What does this all mean for presentations? Often when we are giving a speech or work presentation, we spend a lot of time working on the script or the chart deck. Writing it all out, creating lovely slides to go with it and editing and editing for hours, days even. And we give ourselves minimal time to rehearse it or even say it out loud at all.

This is just wrong.

I'm not saying that the words are not important – of course they are. (I'm going to cover some tips about getting your message across later in the book.) But if you focus exclusively on the words and give no thought to how you will deliver them by using your body and your voice, then you will reduce the impact of your communication *catastrophically*.

The purpose of this book is to give you practical tips and techniques that will help you deliver a smarter presentation. Which means, at some point, you are going to have to practise.

If our body language and voice have a bigger impact than the words, then we must do all we can to get our body and voice awake and ready to perform. But what usually happens is that we go from last-minute slide edits to standing up and presenting – with the result that our communication is, surprise, surprise, low-energy and uninspiring. And we've missed another golden opportunity to build our own reputation.

MAKING YOURSELF HEARD

There are only three things to consider when it comes to making yourself heard – the pitch, the pace and the pause.

1. The pitch is simply the note at which you speak. Just as a musical instrument would be deathly dull if it kept to just one note, the same is true of a speaker if your vocal range is restricted. If your pitch remains 'one note' you fall into monologue – a monotonous drone that makes it hard for the audience to gauge where to pay attention. It's like driving a car in third gear – you'll get there in the end, but it won't get the best out of the engine and it won't sound very pretty. There will be places in your presentation where you'll want to add some light and shade with your voice, to turn the volume up and down, and add variety through emphasis and expression.

Try this:

Out loud, say 'Jack and Jill went up the hill to fetch a pail of water' starting in your usual tone of voice and gradually making your voice go deeper with every word. Notice the different sounds you make and try to drop your voice to be as low as possible with the last word.

Then repeat the sentence but this time start deep and work your way back up the scale so your last word is a high note. Take notice of how you used your breath to deliver the different pitch of each word.

2. The pace is the rate at which you speak. When we're nervous, we tend to speed up in order to race through our presentation and get it done. By rehearsing, you achieve two things: you stop gabbling and racing your words at the beginning because you become aware of yourself, hear the words you're speaking and how they sound; and you can practise where you need to vary the rate at which you speak – in order to add colour and variety to your voice.

A quick canter through the *Guiness Book of Records* reveals that the world's fastest talker, Sean Shannon, can articulate 655 words per minute. Given that the rest of us speak between 125 and 150 words per minute on average, that is extraordinarily pacey and not recommended. During his best speeches, Barack Obama takes it down to 112 wpm.

Part of how quickly you speak will be down to your personal style (once you know that your speed is due to pace not panic). Part of it is the urgency you might want to convey, so it is bound up inextricably with your message (the link between content and tone and body). Just as with writing, using short, sharp words speeds up the pace. Long, polysyllabic words such as erroneous, corrugated, bilateralism and marmalade slow things down. (See what I mean?) An addition of alliteration also aids anti-acceleration – and alliteration can make things memorable, as long as you don't overdo it (like I did here).

Try this:
- **Time yourself**

To get a sense of how long your speech will be, read it out loud in a normal voice with no emphasis or pausing. Time it. Next, read it again. But this time add a beat before you move on to the next paragraph. Slow it right down and time it again. Add the two times up and divide by two and you have a rough indication of your words per minute. But note, aided by adrenaline on the day, you are almost guaranteed to speak faster, so allow for this when planning the length of your speech – come in ahead of your allotted speaking time so that you don't go over.

- **Colour-code your speech**

Go back through your speech and mark up in red, yellow and green where you need to slow right down, where is your 'normal' conversational pace and where you may need to add some speed. The green and the red shouldn't dominate your speech but do need to be there if you want to include some variety to the delivery of your speech

3. The pause is a necessary moment that gives you, the speaker, time to think, gives the audience time to absorb your message and makes you appear confident, authoritative and in control.

A well-deployed pause can also be used for dramatic effect. Again, nerves can stop us from pausing and in fact often the place for the pause is filled with 'ums' and 'ahs'. Resist the temptation to add these 'fillers'. Recognise the pauses for what they are, which is a place to draw breath, take a moment to make eye contact with your audience and let your message land before you move on to the next part of your presentation.

Tip: pausing at the start of your speech or presentation is a great technique to prevent yourself from gabbling the first 30 seconds –

which is what tends to happen when people are a bit nervous. Pausing consciously for a few seconds right at the start doesn't just stop us from gabbling; it also helps the audience re-focus on you, settle down and pay attention. People pay attention to silence. If you don't believe me, cast your mind back to when you were in school and the teacher stopped speaking and fixed you with a gimlet eye. We know who had the power in that little interaction, don't we?

VOLUME CONTROL

We've all met the person with the booming voice who you hear before you see. If the mic breaks when they're presenting, they can immediately raise their volume so people sitting at the back of the room can still hear them. But what happens if you're the quieter type of person? One who depends on the support of technology to be heard and who cannot simply 'project' your voice? What do you do when there is no microphone, but you need to be heard across the boardroom table, classroom or town hall? You want your audience to be focused on what you're saying, not straining to hear every word.

Here, breath is your friend and, if this is you, you're probably not making the most effective use of it. Breathy speech is inefficient and can show a lack of support from the rest of your body (as well as betraying – consciously or otherwise – a lack of belief in your content). By gently engaging your abdominal muscles when you are speaking and gently releasing them when you are breathing in, you'll help to maintain breath pressure and produce a clearer sound as a result.

Try this:
Hold your hand in front of your face and exhale gently so you feel your breath on your hand. Notice what happens in your stomach – your lower abdomen contracts, gently 'pushing' the breath from your body. Now, using the same amount of breath and the same amount

of abdominal pressure, gently say, 'Hello'. Sounds almost like a whisper, doesn't it?

Now repeat with a little more breath. Keep your hand at arm's length, work the abdominal muscles a bit harder and use a little more breath and your gentle 'hello' will be a little louder. Imagine someone is sitting at the end of the boardroom table or across the classroom or even the end of a long room. For each position, send the breath to reach them. Notice the work your abdominal muscles are doing and replicate that work with your voice: 'Hello.'

You may be surprised by the amount of breath and abdominal work that is needed to be audible over the different distances. But don't be tempted to use too much breath and abdominal pressure to force the words out – you don't want to sound forced or strained.

Allow the size of the room and the placement of your audience to inform the volume of air you take in and the effort you need to engage to make your voice heard. That way you'll always be audible, and you'll never be hoarse.

REASON – A CAUTIONARY TALE

You can create impact for the wrong reasons too. Here are some real-life examples that will make you feel better about yourself as they didn't happen to you.

- The VIP client was called by the wrong name not once, but all the way through the presentation. Sorry Clare, I mean, Kate.
- The MD decided to 'open up' the presentation with a gushing welcome of why this client was so interesting and important. When the client leant over, turned off the projector and said, 'Don't worry about the presentation; tell me what you think we should do with our business', the MD had nothing to say because he hadn't been to any

of the rehearsals, hadn't read the brief and had no idea what was required.

- My boss managed to step into a wastepaper bin – or trash can – get it stuck on his foot and couldn't get it off. To this day, I have no idea how it happened and yet I will never forget it (unlike the presentation he eventually made, which failed to make any impression at all).

5.
Mission

'A mission is not about changing the world,
but about changing yourself.'
UNKNOWN

The word 'mission' comes from a Latin word that means 'to send'. It's an appropriate word for presenting, where you are sending your message out into the world, wanting it to land with your audience and provoke a reaction. It's a dynamic word, a reminder of the need for something to happen as a result of your communication – making your audience think, feel and do differently.

TELLING YOUR STORY

Research by Thomas Graeber, assistant professor of business administration at Harvard Business School, found that audiences are more likely to recall information over a longer period of time when it is shared as an anecdote rather than a set of statistics.[3]

Instinctively, this makes sense. Stories tend to be more interesting than charts, slide decks and reams of statistics. However, the reason we recall them more easily is not necessarily because stories are more inspirational or persuasive. It is because of how our memory works.

Graeber's research looked at how quickly the effect of different types of information on beliefs fades over time. He found that, while the effect of a story faded by roughly a third over the course of a

---

[3] https://hbswk.hbs.edu/item/looking-to-leave-mark-memorable-leaders-tell-stories-dont-spout-statistics.

single day, the effect of a statistic faded by a much more dramatic 73 per cent.

The study found that stories live longer in our memories because they are more likely to include distinctive details or context that aids recall. In contrast, because statistics and numbers are abstract constructs, they can be harder for the human brain to recall.

So what are the ingredients for a great story?

Let's go back in time for some help from the Ancient Greeks.

Aristotle was a philosopher and polymath who founded the Peripatetic school of philosophy at the Lyceum in Athens. It was he who defined rhetoric – the art of persuasion, which, along with grammar and logic, is one of the three ancient arts of discourse. Rhetoric is concerned with the techniques that speakers and writers use to inform, persuade or motivate particular audiences in specific situations. As such, it's useful to understand if we want to be better at presenting.

Rhetoric provides a mental shortcut to simplify problems and make it easier to understand, discover and develop arguments. The most famous example of the 'rhetorical triangle' is logos, pathos and ethos – Aristotle's three persuasive appeals to an audience.

Logos appeals to reason. It can also be thought of as the text of the argument, as well as how well you argue your point.

Ethos appeals to your character. Here, it's about your role in the argument – how credible you are.

Pathos appeals to the emotions and the sympathetic imagination, as well as to beliefs and values. Pathos can also be thought of as the role of the audience in the argument – their response to you.

And there's a fourth mode of persuasion – **kairos** – which means 'right time' or 'opportunity'. It's an appeal to the context or timeliness in which the presentation is given, which may have an impact on the audience's reception to your argument or message.

- This could include the time at which the presentation is taking place. For example, if it's after lunch and you are in a darkened conference room with no natural light, you're going to have to be very high energy to keep the audience with you.
- It could be the occasion: formal or informal? Sombre or joyful?
- It could reflect something relevant or important that has just happened in the last few days.

Kairos also reflects the background information and demographics of an audience, such as age, culture, faith, creed, etc.; the appropriateness of the speaker's tone given the nature of the occasion; and the relationship between the speaker, the audience and the topic.

For example, I recently read a souvenir book celebrating 150 years of Henley Royal Regatta. It was published in 1989. The then Chairman of the regatta was being interviewed and was asked why there were no races for women at the regatta. His response, 'That question bores me', elicited no follow-up response from the journalist. The chairman's dismissive stance was par for the course thirty-plus years ago. The majority view then was that women athletes had no place at Henley Royal Regatta, an argument that has not aged well by today's mores (and, fortunately, is no longer the reality).

If that interview was repeated in 2023 with the same person, who had the same credentials (ethos), and who used the same arguments made with the same logic (logos), and they both made appeal to the same emotions and the same values (pathos), but the *reception* is completely different, then what has changed is the *context* in which the statement was made (kairos). In this scenario, it's highly unlikely that the Chairman's response would go unchallenged by a journalist today. More likely, that statement would become the main story – the journalist would scent a scoop and ask lots more follow-up questions to expose the Chair's sexist attitudes.

So what does all this Greek history mean for us in the twenty-first century as we put our presentations together? It's another handy checklist to ensure we're doing all we can to persuade our audience to join our mission.

Ask yourself:

Logos – *What's the core of my argument, the logic of the case I'm making?* What are you trying to persuade your audience to think, feel, do?

Ethos – *Have I explained why I am qualified to make this case?* You don't need to include a lengthy CV or resumé but you will need to share some aspect of your experience that is relevant. For example, it could be that you've been working in this particular field for decades or you are the leader of the team working on the project or the author of the research.

Pathos – *Have I added some 'colour'?* What anecdotes or stories can you tell to bring your argument to life?

Kairos – *Is there a particular timeliness to my speech?* This could be the time of day you are presenting but it could also be timeliness of content. For example, you are giving a speech about the need for more consistent government investment in the arts the day after the government has announced its eleventh culture secretary in a decade.

For inspiration, watch BBC News as it does this so well. Let's take the example of the annual budget announcement:

Logos – The core of the argument is to persuade the audience that the BBC's reporters are providing an unbiased account of the key implications of the budget announcement.

Ethos – The reporter, an experienced journalist, will interview an economist, an independent expert.

Pathos – After the studio interview, which has been illustrated with some key charts and data, we move to an interview of a couple in their local corner shop talking about the 'real world' impact the budget will have on their cost of living. This contextualises and humanises the budget and data.

Kairos – The report is timely, because the budget was announced in Parliament earlier that day.

Other ingredients for a great story

Main character energy

Who's at the heart of your story? Is it you, someone else, the brand, your customers, your employees? Whoever is the main protagonist, they are the one driving the story forward and we experience the story from their point of view.

Conflict

What was the initial challenge? What obstacles were overcome? Who was the common enemy? Great stories have an element of conflict to add some grit to the oyster. If everything is straightforward or easy, it's a dull story.

Magic
What did you/the main character do that was different, clever or special? What were the advantages you gained as a result?

Involvement
You don't want to turn your presentation into a free for all, but some judicious audience participation can help remove the barriers between them and you, and make them feel more involved in your story.

Emotion
Some laughs, tears, outrage – emotions are convincing. The audience acts as a mirror to your performance; if you are showing emotion, it's likely they'll feel it too. People in business are too often scared of emotion. They hold themselves in check far too readily. No one is advocating you use extreme emotions (unless there's a fire in the building in which case, shout loud and with urgency!). But in the right place, the right level of emotion can be very compelling.

Surprise
When stories surprise us, they keep us hooked and wanting to hear more. Thrillers do this particularly well by ending each chapter with a cliff-hanger that makes you want to turn the page and find out what happens next. It should be the same for your presentation – what happens next? Tell me more!

STEAL WITH PRIDE – THE PIXAR APPROACH
One of my clients was a global multinational packaged goods company that manufactured and sold a huge range of products from washing powder to toothpaste. It had a mantra for innovation: 'steal with pride'. What this meant was not corporate espionage – spying on competitors and stealing their best ideas. No, it was more that you

should take inspiration from another product line or category and see if you could apply some of the thinking to your own product or category. For example, fabric conditioners came in a range of scents from vanilla to lavender but for many years washing-up liquid was only available in one scent. By taking inspiration from the world of washing clothes, washing dishes is now an olfactory experience too. So, in the same vein, why not look at some of the best storytellers in the world and take inspiration from them?

If I asked you to think of a company that is renowned for creating films with compelling and emotionally engaging stories you'd quickly come up with Pixar. It famously uses a set of principles and techniques to create consistently compelling and commercially successful films. Here are a few key elements of its approach, which might inspire you to do something similar in your own presentation. Go ahead, 'steal with pride'.

The *What if?* question: Many Pixar films start with a simple question that serves as the core concept of the story. For example, 'What if toys had feelings?' (*Toy Story*) or 'What if emotions had emotions?' (*Inside Out*).

How could you use the 'what if?' technique to reframe the issue or the audience's perception of the subject being discussed in your presentation? What metaphor could make the complicated concept you want to talk about really simple for your audience to understand?

Unexpected twists: Pixar often incorporates unexpected twists in their storytelling to keep audiences engaged and surprised. These twists can subvert common storytelling conventions and challenge characters in unique ways.

How could you insert a surprise plot twist to your presentation to re-engage the audience at the most dense part of your presentation? For example, could you insert a relevant but funny slide or a cartoon to give them a break from the bar charts and graphs? If you are doing your presentation with someone else in your team, can you hand over to them (a new character) to bring a new voice into the room and a different perspective? This sort of dynamic on stage can really enliven a serious presentation.

Nostalgia and nostalgic references: Pixar movies frequently include cultural references and nods to their own films. These elements create a sense of nostalgia for the audience while also enhancing the interconnectedness of the Pixar universe.

You could be presenting in an historic venue or talking to an audience who have a different culture to your own. Or perhaps you are following on from a presentation you did the previous year to the same audience. Get the audience onside by using their language – at least to say hello and goodbye and thank you – or by referencing their cultural calendar rather than your own.

Strong visual themes: Visual motifs and recurring symbols can help unify a film's narrative and provide deeper layers of meaning. These visual cues can reinforce the themes and emotions of the story. How can you use imagery and symbolism to underscore your story? Can you keep returning to a common theme or use a visual analogy to progress your narrative? I have used the well-known image of a Trojan horse to explain my approach to helping people make better presentations. Like the Ancient Greeks finding a way to get inside the city of Troy unseen, my techniques help your message to get inside the heads of your audience – and, just like Odysseus, you will also get the result you want.

Surreal elements: Incorporating surreal or fantastical elements into storytelling allows Pixar to explore the boundaries of imagination and creativity. Using unconventional storytelling techniques brings in the different, and different holds an audience's attention.

Why not break a few rules when it comes to presenting? For example, many presenters use stock photography and imagery in hope that a picture of a group of people smiling and shaking hands with each other in an office environment adds warmth and humanity to their charts. Or that a picture of someone punching the air in victory signals achievement or success. Actually, stock imagery is just that: stock. Visual cliché. It doesn't engage the audience because they have seen it so many times before. It fails to surprise. How much better to be brave and use one of your own photos to make a point. Or use a prop – hold something up that makes the audience think or wonder or see something in a new way.

Music and sound: The use of music and sound design is vital to creating atmosphere, emotion and pacing in Pixar films. Memorable scores and well-chosen songs contribute to the overall impact of the storytelling.

How can you use sound or music to enliven your presentation? Can you use music for your entrance on stage or when you reveal your big point? You could make a short film showing your team collaborating on the project with a music soundtrack to convey fun and dynamism at work. A note of caution when using 'walk on' music. It has to be appropriate for the venue. Booming music when getting onto a large conference stage is fine. Booming music when walking into a meeting room, less so. Just ask David Brent.

Stakes and consequences: Establishing high stakes and meaningful consequences for characters' actions adds tension and urgency to the plot. This can make the audience more invested in the outcome. If you are telling your story, your journey to giving this presentation, help the audience feel the highs and lows of the process of getting here. TED Talk speakers often use their own story or the story of someone they worked with or know. Individual stories are powerful and, often, the stakes are high. Share them.

Silent moments: Pixar recognises the power of silence in storytelling. Moments without dialogue can convey emotions and character relationships through visual cues and body language. When we present, we often confuse talking for communicating. But, as we have already seen, words are only part of the communication process. Most presenters forget to use silence or pauses to punctuate their prose. But silence can be laden with meaning – disapproval, drama, suspense, anticipation of a punchline. See what I mean? (Cue silence so you can digest that.)

Pacing and rhythm: Varying the pacing and rhythm of a film can evoke different emotions and maintain the audience's interest throughout the story. Same for us. We've discussed using short, sharp words to pick up the pace and longer, polysyllabic words to slow things down. Sometimes you want to convey urgency – speed up. Other times you want to communicate calm or reflectiveness – slow the pace down. Too much speed is exhausting for the audience (think too many action sequences in a film but no dialogue). Too slow and it's boring for the audience. We need variety of energy to stay engaged.

Humour for all ages: Pixar films often include humour that appeals to both children and adults so that viewers of all ages can find moments to enjoy. If you're making a wedding speech, better not be too sombre or serious. But remember it's a family occasion so there needs to be stuff in the speech for all ages. At a town hall, you need to relate to everyone from the shop floor to the C-suite. A light touch of humour leavens any situation and, even if the message you're delivering is hard for people to hear, gentle humour might help you appear more human and make the pain more bearable.

A CAUTIONARY TALE

September 2023. A few days before the end of the summer holidays, it was found that over a hundred UK schools were in danger of collapse as they were constructed from reinforced autoclaved aerated concrete (RAAC), a lightweight form of concrete that's weaker than normal building material.

As more and more schools closed due to RAAC, the prime minister, Rishi Sunak, was accused of making school-repair budget cuts during his time as Chancellor of the Exchequer.

Education secretary Gillian Keegan went on ITV News to defend the government. Unfortunately for her, she forgot the first rule of media interviews: you are always on. She was recorded on camera suggesting others 'have been sat on their arses' over the RAAC crisis – while saying publicly in the interview that the government should be thanked for their speedy response.

In the moments after the main body of the interview had finished, and as the camera repositioned for extra shots, Keegan – still wearing her microphone – criticised others and claimed the government had gone 'over and above' what could have been expected in addressing concerns relating to RAAC.

'Does anyone ever say, "You know what, you've done a f***ing good job, because everyone else has sat on their arses and done nothing"?' Ms Keegan asked.

She added: 'Any sign of that? No?'

Naturally, it was this part of the 'interview' that went viral, not her 'on the record' response. The moral of this story being, keep your off-the-cuff comments to yourself until you are sure you are in a place of safety. Walls, lifts, taxi drivers, receptionists and camera people all have ears – assume they are listening and keep schtum!

6.
Energy

'The best way to conquer stage fright is to know
what you're talking about.'
MICHAEL H. MESCON

Remember Dolly Parton? She has energy. You probably know people like her – they're often described as 'bubbly'. They are the human equivalent of that school chemistry experiment when potassium is added to water: the metal melts and floats. It whizzes around very quickly on the surface of the water then self-ignites, which results in sparks and a lilac flame. Dramatic. Exciting. Showy.

Reader, as you may have gathered by now, I am not like that.

But that's not to say that I can't deliver a presentation with energy. And if you err on the non-bubbly side too, it doesn't mean that you can't either. If you are not a naturally effervescent character, all it means is that you have to work a bit harder. A good starting point is to focus on dealing with any nerves that might get in the way given that, for non-bubbly people, nervous energy can turn us even more introverted, even more dead-pan and, I'm sorry to say, even more bad-tempered. All behaviours that get in the way of building warm rapport with our audience.

DEALING WITH NERVES

When our brain perceives a threat, we automatically react with one of four trauma responses, depending on our individual past experiences of trauma. For many of us, the thought of standing in front of an audience provides the same adrenaline rush as the thought of being chased by a bull in a field. We don't relish the prospect and we're terrified of how we might react. As a result, even though logically we know that giving a presentation is a non-threatening situation, our trauma responses could be activated.

By exploring what each response entails and the thoughts and behaviours associated with each response, we can face the fear. We can apply some useful techniques to help cope with those overactive and distracting trauma responses that can get in the way of delivering a great presentation.

THE FIGHT RESPONSE
Protecting yourself from threat through conflict.

If you tend towards the fight response, you're likely to believe that if you establish power over the threat, it will result in security and control. This response may feel like an adrenaline rush, along with a desire to defend yourself through fighting, yelling at, or controlling others. The driving thought behind this response is *I need to eliminate the threat before it eliminates me.* You might be familiar with some of these behaviours as you are preparing your speech or presentation or while you are delivering it, which indicate this trauma response:

- Crying
- Hands in fists, desire to punch
- Flexed/tight jaw, grinding teeth
- Fight in eyes, glaring, fight in voice
- Desire to stomp, kick, smash with legs, feet
- Feelings of anger/rage
- Knotted stomach/nausea, burning stomach

THE FLIGHT RESPONSE
Protecting yourself from threat through escape.
People in the midst of a flight response often report difficulties with relaxation and sitting still as they are constantly worrying, rushing, hiding or panicking when they feel threatened. The thought behind the response is *I need to run from the situation before it can hurt me.* If you are familiar with these types of behaviour before and during your presentation, you're in flight mode:

- Restless legs, feet
- Numbness in legs
- Anxiety, shallow breathing
- Big/darting eyes
- Leg/foot movement
- Reported or observed fidgety-ness, restlessness, feeling trapped

THE FREEZE RESPONSE
Protecting yourself from threat through dissociation.
This is the one many of us have dreamt of in the run up to an important presentation. We're on stage, looking out at the audience and suddenly we cannot think of what to say, our mouth won't open to get the words out and we have 'frozen'. It's the trauma response that unconsciously detaches us from the situation by 'freezing' or spacing out. Our body can feel rigid and stressed. Even if we don't freeze on stage, this way of dealing with perceived danger (the upcoming presentation) may result in difficulty making decisions or getting motivated. So we put off preparing and practising because the thought behind this response is, *If I don't do anything, the threat cannot hurt me.* It comes from the same place as the client I mentioned earlier who didn't want to rehearse because then he had an excuse for being terrible.

If this is you, you'll be familiar with these behaviours:

- Feeling stuck in some part of the body
- Feeling cold/frozen, numb, pale skin
- Sense of stiffness, heaviness
- Holding breath/restricted breathing
- Sense of dread, heart pounding

THE FAWN RESPONSE

Protecting yourself from threat through placation.

I often see this come to the fore in business pitches or Q&A sessions. If you tend to the fawn response, it's likely that you avoid conflict or deal with it through people-pleasing. You might find it difficult to say no to clients and colleagues. You're afraid to say what you really think or feel because you don't want to upset anyone and you don't want anyone to disagree with you. The danger is you are so accommodating of other's needs that you tend to ignore your own. And this response is dangerous when stating your case in a pitch or a presentation as you're likely to undermine your case by caving to the first person who asks a challenging question.

The thought behind this response is, *If I can appease this person, I can be safe from conflict or pain.* Check this list and see if you recognise any of these behaviours.

- Over-apologising to others
- Difficulty saying no
- Excessive flattery of the other person
- Going out of the way to please others
- Neglecting one's own needs
- Always agreeing with others even when you don't (avoiding conflict)

HOW TO COPE

When it comes to presenting, your fight, flight or freeze responses will show themselves in the adrenaline racing around your body, which will affect your physiology and your breath in different ways – whether that's taking shallow breaths, having knots in your stomach, pacing, fidgeting or standing rooted to the spot in rigid terror. Breaking news: it's highly unlikely these feelings and behaviours will go away. Nerves are natural; they show you care about what you are doing and that it is important to you. But what you can do is make sure that you make the adrenaline *work for you* rather than distract you.

BREATHWORK

Often, nerves show themselves in our voice, either by our breath 'disappearing' as we run out of air or through a dry and raspy – or squeaky – voice. Practising 'good' breathing will help you control your voice and help with both how you feel (relaxed) and your voice projection.

Get to know the mechanics of your breathing and aim for your breath to be deep and even.

When we breathe in, our ribs move up and out and our diaphragm flattens. Air is drawn into the lungs through the nose and the lungs expand until the whole chest space is filled with air. The chest should expand in all directions.

When we breathe out, the chest wall and diaphragm return to their original position and air is forced out of the lungs. The muscles in between the ribs control how quickly the ribs and lungs collapse.

If you notice your ribs are rapidly moving up and down, it's likely your breathing is too shallow. Slow the breath down until you feel it coming from your belly rather than your throat. Beware also of raising your shoulders – they should not be moving at all.

BREATHING EXERCISES

Place your hands lightly on your ribs and breathe in and out to a count of three. Keep your shoulders down – they should not be lifting as you breathe.

Repeat the exercise, breathing in to the count of three and out to five.

When you are comfortable with this, try breathing in for the count of three and then, as you breathe out, speak out loud the days of the week – literally saying, 'Monday, Tuesday, Wednesday, Thursday, Friday, Saturday, Sunday' as slowly as you can with the aim of getting to the end of the week without running out of breath.

RELAXATION EXERCISES

If you really struggle with nerves, you need to get into the habit of relaxing. This sounds counterintuitive, but understanding how your body feels when you are stressed and anxious will also help you understand how to become familiar with the difference between a relaxed and a tense body.

Let's release our inner yoga instructor, get down on the floor and try these exercises:

Exercise 1

Lie flat on the floor. Clench each muscle in turn until your whole body is tense and tight. Slowly count to five and gently release the tension so you feel your muscles relaxing. Become aware of the difference between your tense body and your relaxed body. Note where you carry tension – often we hunch our shoulders without even realising it.

Exercise 2

Stand with your feet slightly wider than your shoulders and your hands held loosely by your sides. Concentrate on your breathing, listening to the sound as the breath is taken into your body and then released. Breathe in through your nose counting to three, then breathe out through your mouth counting to three again. Slow your breathing right down until you reach a rhythmical pattern.

Exercise 3

Stand up straight and then let your body flop downwards from the waist. Let your body hang loosely for a few seconds and enjoy the rush of blood to your head. Gently raise your body upright again and breathe deeply and calmly, saying to yourself, 'I am relaxed. I am relaxed. I am relaxed.'

Exercise 4

Mouth the letters 'O' ... 'E' ... 'O' ... 'E' silently, opening your mouth as wide as you can each time.

WARMING UP

You need to warm up. Anyone who plays sports, goes running or does any kind of physical exercise is familiar with the warm-up (and cool down) that happens at the start (and end) of each session. And yet, in business, we go into presentations cold, our minds elsewhere, our bodies either rigid with nerves or sweating with adrenaline. Warming up gets you into 'state', moves the adrenaline around your body, and enables you to start your presentation physically prepared and ready.

You don't need to spend hours on your warm-up, you just need to do *something*. You know your body – what it responds well to and also its limitations. So proceed sensibly and don't strain; just be comfortable. You're not trying to win the Olympics, just to limber up and energise your body to prepare for performance.

Try these:

- **Shake it out.** Stand up with your feet shoulder-width apart and let your hands drop to your sides. Shake your right arm as hard as you can and then let it drop to your side again. It should feel tingly and alive, especially in comparison to the other arm which probably has all the energy of a discarded tree branch. So shake that left arm out too. Move on to your legs – give them a shake, one after the other. Bring in the hips – evoke the spirit of primary school PE classes and put your hands on your hips and rotate them round. Bend over at the waist to get the blood rushing to your head. Jog on the spot. You get the idea. Do something physical with your body so you wake it up.

- **Swim with your shoulders.** Your shoulders are important too and often hold tension. Relax and roll your shoulders, stretch and yawn, go swimming on dry land with some front crawl, breaststroke or backstroke with your arms to open up your shoulders. Lift your shoulders up to your ears and drop them down again – do it five times. Feel the tension dissipate.

- **Manipulate your neck.** Looking straight ahead, gently turn your head to look over your right shoulder. Bring your head back to the centre and then turn your head to look over your left shoulder. Bring it back to the centre and drop your head so your chin is on your chest.

- **Open your mouth.** When we are tense and nervous our jaw muscles tighten, which means we don't open our mouths enough, we don't articulate our words and we end up mumbling or swallowing our words. With your fingers, find the big muscle that holds your jaw together at the side of your face. Open your mouth and, using your fingers, give that muscle some love – massage it gently to warm it up.

- **Pretend you are chewing a sticky toffee** (or have a real one if you fancy it). Get that jaw moving – forget everything you know about not eating with your mouth open, we need to see that mouth opening as wide as it can go.

- **Wake up your eyes**. Many of us struggle to get a good night's sleep ahead of a big presentation and our eyes can be a giveaway that we didn't get our allotted eight hours. With your fingers, gently massage the skin around your eyes – to the sides and gently underneath. Open them up wide, roll them around and rapidly flutter your eyelashes to wake up the lids. Alternatively, rub your palms together very fast and then place the fleshy part of each hand over each eye. You will feel the warmth transmit from your palms to your eyes, which makes them feel good.

- **Scrumple your face.** We have twenty flat skeletal muscles in our faces. Some of us are naturally more animated than others. If you know that your 'resting face' has all the animation of an Easter Island statue, you're going to have to work a bit harder on waking it up and showing expression. Do your widest, cheesiest, toothy grin. Scrumple your face like a piece of paper then stretch and scrumple it several times. Hate this? Make like Munch and do a silent scream – open your mouth and eyes as wide as possible so it feels like your cheekbones are going to hit your eyelids. And relax.

Do them all or do some of them, run up the stairs, power walk around the block, play some uplifting music whilst you jump up and down on the spot and pretend you're Rocky Balboa – whatever you do, do some sort of physical activity. You'll feel alive and ready for action if you do. And you'll think faster on your feet, too, because an awake body creates a more alert mind. (It's why stand-up comedians warm up – that way they're prepared for any hecklers and can come back at them quick as a flash.)

And if you're nervous about being seen doing all of these in the office or conference venue, find a quiet corner or go into the toilets and stretch out there. It only takes a minute or so to wake your body up. And if you're presenting on screen, it's even more important to warm up. On screen, the participants in the call only have your voice energy to keep them engaged. And your voice energy will be much more impactful if your body is warmed up ready to support it. TV presenters exude controlled energy – even news anchors, who need to radiate calm and control.

Then there's your voice. What can you do to ensure the first sound that comes out of your mouth is not a timorous squeak? Try these:

- **Breathe deeply.** Concentrate on breathing down to the bottom of your lungs and don't let your shoulders rise up. Let the lungs expand all around so that you allow yourself to relax and take breaths that get down to the bottom of your lungs to get the most capacity. Really focus on your breathing. When we get nervous, it's our breath that often gives us away, we forget to breathe, we carry on talking and we run out of air. Instead, use the warm-up to breathe deeply, to focus your mind on your presentation. Imagine yourself on stage – confident, articulate and at ease. You know your stuff. You are ready.

- **Warm up your voice.** A strange thing happens when my sister and I get together. We start talking and immediately it sounds like we have a frog in our throats and each has to do a lot of throat-clearing and coughing to start speaking clearly again. Why? I have no idea, but I see it happening to other people about to present too so I need to take my own medicine next time I see her and try these:

- **Practise tongue twisters.** We get lazy with our articulation and can tail off at the end of a sentence or mumble or drop syllables. Tongue twisters are designed to trip us up and yet, if we really articulate the words, we can get the better of them. Try these:

Repeat at least ten times:

'Unique New York'

'Red lorry, yellow lorry'

'Red leather, yellow leather'

'Peggy Babcock'

'Whether the weather is cold or whether the weather is hot, we'll weather the weather, whatever the weather, whether we like it or not.'

'The lips, the teeth, the tip of the tongue, the tip of the tongue, the teeth, the lips.'

These tongue twisters will put energy and expression into

your voice and help to make the most of your vocal range. They'll also get your mouth warmed up and ready.

I can't be certain but I'm pretty sure it was Jerry Seinfeld who said that, after listening to a recording of his own voice he wanted to apologise to everyone he had ever spoken to in his life. But, if we want to improve our presentation skills, we need to get comfortable with hearing our own voice and doing all we can to prime it for peak performance.

What else can you do to warm up the voice?

- **Hum a tune and then speak the first minute of your presentation out loud.** Or read a paragraph from a book with no intonation and then with some energy and emphasis, and be aware of how you're making your voice work. Record it on your phone and play it back. What do you like? What could you improve?

- **Alter the volume, variety and pitch of your voice to give more music and interest to the sound you make**. Your voice is your musical instrument. You can hold the listener's attention by adding interest to it by altering the pitch and tone of your voice. Where are the places you need to add volume? Where you are saying with your voice tone, 'Hey, sit up and take notice of this?'

WHAT CAN I DO IF I HAVE TO SPEAK ON AN EMOTIONAL SUBJECT, BUT I DON'T WANT TO CHOKE, CRY OR STUMBLE?

Sometimes we're not making a presentation to the board, we are delivering a eulogy or a vote of thanks to someone we care deeply about. The topic matter is emotional, the venue may be intimidating, and you may be feeling under a great deal of stress because you have recently dealt with a life-changing situation, such as the death of a loved one.

Here's a technique that involves tying the thought to the breath in such a way that the thought fails to activate your fight, flight, freeze or fawn response on the day.

Isolate the tricky piece and practise it in a variety of circumstances – while driving, while running, while climbing stairs, saying it with a 'laugh' in your voice (it will feel weird, but go with it).

Then rehearse your eulogy in front of a mirror or your computer screen having previously pasted a photo of a similar-looking audience to your actual audience. (You can download a generic image from Google.)

The more you practise and repeat your speech, the more this will prevent nerves from triggering the choke breath, which activates the fight, flight, freeze or fawn response. Repeating the speech before your audience photo slide will trick your brain into thinking you've done 'this old thing' a million times before.

Even with this preparation, you may still stumble and get choked up on the day. Take a big breath. Pause. Gather and go again. Focus only on the message itself. Be kind to yourself – your audience will know how hard this is for you. They will be empathetic. Showing some vulnerability and emotion is expected and will only show you care.

ANOTHER CONFIDENCE 'TRICK'

Often, just before you go 'on stage' is the most nerve-wracking part of your presentation. Once you get going, having nailed your ABCD, the tension dissipates and you can even start to enjoy yourself. But, when you're waiting for your turn to speak, heart racing and sweaty of palm, 'enjoying it' feels an impossible task.

Here's a technique that will help you 'get into state' – ready to be the top performer that everyone has the potential to be. It's called, 'Act as if' and, don't worry, no theatre skills are required.

Begin by imagining you are Alexandria Ocasio-Cortez, also known by her initials AOC, the American politician and activist. Taking office at age twenty-nine, Ocasio-Cortez is the youngest woman ever to serve in the United States Congress, following what was widely seen as the biggest upset victory in the 2018 midterm election primaries when she defeated Democratic Caucus Chair Joe Crowley, a ten-term incumbent. If you haven't seen AOC give a speech, make haste to YouTube and look her up – she is incredibly impressive.

Now you have a picture of her in your mind, imagine you are her and your audience is waiting for you to speak. Would they be excited? Interested? Curious? As soon as you step on the stage, would the room fall silent in anticipation? Of course it would.

And then, what if you decided to 'Act as if' you were AOC or even just the piece of her that you particularly admired – perhaps it's how she is so articulate with no ums and ahs when she speaks. Perhaps it is her wide smile and the pleasure she often shows when she is communicating with others, or perhaps it is her steely determination to stand up for the causes she believes in. Think yourself into that mode. You'll find that you naturally exude more confidence and feel more relaxed.

Quite often, when we take on a part or a role, it's easier to channel that person's style and energy. In workshops, we often get people to take names of famous people out of a hat and ask them to behave like that person at a party meeting other people. With everyone in the room assuming the character of a famous person – from the iconic jazz singer Josephine Baker through to Albert Einstein – everyone comes alive and the conversation flows.

Who would be a good role model for you? Who do you admire? This is not about abandoning your authentic self, but it is about 'borrowing' the attributes of others to think differently about yourself in order to get over those first few seconds of nerves and angst.

Alternatively, you can use this approach in a more simple way. It's all about affirmations.

Positive affirmations are simple statements that shift your mindset from self-criticism and negativity to focusing on your strengths and being positive about yourself. Do they work? Well, according to a study published in the journal *Psychological Science* in 2016, the answer is yes.[4] Apparently, positive affirmations activate your brain's reward system and alleviate some of the stress you might have felt otherwise. Just the process of replacing negative or anxious thoughts with positivity can help relax and calm your body.

And, what's most helpful for overcoming pre-presentation nerves is that our brains can't always tell the difference between reality and imagination, so when you regularly repeat affirming statements, it leads your brain to be convinced that your visions are fact, which then leads you to believe you can do better.

You don't have to be David Brent from *The Office*, looking into a mirror and saying, 'I'm a tiger' – although please do if you think it would help – but saying a few positive statements before you begin your presentation is another way of getting into state and ensuring you're in a front-footed frame of mind.

This is the type of affirmation that some people find helpful:

– My presentation is brilliant – I can't wait to share it
– This information is helpful to my audience
– People are here because they are interested in hearing what I have to say

---

[4] J. M. Dutcher, et al, 'Self-Affirmation Activates the Ventral Striatum: A Possible Reward-Related Mechanism for Self-Affirmation', *Psychological Science*, 2016, 27(4).

– I have the skills and abilities to handle this situation
– I am confident and ready to start
– I am powerful and confident
– I trust myself and follow my instincts
– I am articulate and well prepared
– I am ready

But if that all sounds totally woo woo and cringe then forget about affirmations and just say to yourself, 'I can do this' – because you can. I still remember the feeling I had many years ago when I was alone in a dingy hotel room in Prague, the night before I was due to give a workshop to a group of executives. I was rehearsing my opening remarks out loud and every time I did it, I tripped over my words or forgot the key point or tuned into the sound of my voice and hated it. I remember lying down on the bed staring at the ceiling in a state of abject panic – 'I am going to be utterly, utterly crap and I have come all this way and it is going to be so embarrassing.'

And then I decided to chant a few affirmations. Actually, no, I didn't. Affirmations hadn't been invented then and, even if they had, I think I would have felt massively self-conscious saying, 'I am articulate and well prepared,' as the evidence of my rehearsal was showing very much to the contrary. However, what I did was trust myself. I knew that, however crap my rehearsal was (and it was really crap), just the very fact that I had rehearsed time and again meant that on the day it would go well. Because it had happened before and I had to trust that it would again. And, guess what? It did go well. My opening remarks were strong, once I got into the workshop element I responded to the people's comments on the day and the whole event was a success. Trust yourself. As long as you prepare and rehearse – you can do this.

RESPONDING TO THE AUDIENCE

Imagine the scenario. You're in the middle of your presentation. You started strong, felt confident and yet, ten minutes in you look across the audience and see some blank faces. So many blank faces. And that person there – she's frowning. Yikes! Suddenly you feel really self-conscious. Doubt enters your mind. All that preparation and planning and they hate what you're saying. What to do?

Your first inclination could be to end this horrific experience as quickly as possible. Speed up what you're saying and get the hell out of Dodge. But on second thought, no – let's try to make this work. It's time to engage with the audience. Here are some ideas that can help turn the situation around when you think that you may have lost your audience's attention.

Keep your confidence and engage your energy. Don't panic! You may be misreading the signals. When I'm watching TV at home, my 'resting face' is completely blank. I may be watching the most fascinating, most compelling, most disturbing or most intriguing piece of television or cinema and you would never be able to tell from my face whether I loved it or hated it. Many people simply don't animate their faces when they are listening to others. The exception to this is a response to humour. You will see immediately whether your hilarious remark has got the audience in fits of laughter or totally missed the mark. But for everything else, the audience may be simply reflecting on what you're saying and taking it all in. Even if they do hate it, you will gain nothing by losing energy and self-confidence halfway through your presentation. Sometimes the best strategy is to keep going. And keep going as if you believe the audience thinks this is the greatest thing they have ever heard. Perhaps it is.

Know the audience culture. For many years, the consumer goods giant, P&G, was my company's most valued client. When we did good work, it opened the door for other projects but because P&G is scrupulously fair, despite us being an 'agency of record', we would always have to pitch for new work. On this occasion, we were pitching to lead a communications campaign for a new line of washing powder. We entered the room and saw that the pitch panel consisted of three long-standing clients who we had worked with on projects over the past few years. We had good relationships with these people – or so we thought – and yet, there they sat, stoney-faced, not looking particularly engaged. Yikes! However, we were aware that it was the company's policy for their people to not give any reaction to sales pitches. It didn't make it particularly easy, but it did mean we kept our energy up, we presented as if we were getting an enthusiastic and heartfelt response instead of blank stares and we won the pitch. Having an understanding of the culture and approach was useful intelligence that ensured we were not put off our stride on the day.

Different cultures – not just company cultures, but social and societal ones too – create different ways for audiences to behave. Take your audience's culture into account. In the USA, audiences can be more participative and open to involvement. Some Asian audiences won't want audience participation and may listen with their eyes closed so as to concentrate better on what is being said. They aren't asleep. They're listening intently.

Ask an open question. Pause and check in with the audience. Ask them if this all makes sense and are they with you so far. No lawyer would ask in court a question that they don't know the answer to, but here is the chance to get some debate going midstream. Questions to ask in order to get concerns out in the open:

– 'It looks like not everyone agrees. Would anyone like to share their view?'

– 'Do you think what I am saying is right or wrong? What have I missed?'

If you take this approach you have to host the debate without being defensive. Or you could acknowledge that not everyone agrees but ask them to hear your case to the end and then debate it at the end.

Listen hard and adapt. If you are presenting to the board, your boss or your client and they've just told you they don't want to hear all the details but do want to focus on a particular point – you need to change tack. Resist the temptation to plough on because you've done all this work and you damn well want to show you've done it. Talk to the points they want and need. The only exception to this is when you know that you won't be able to get the decision you need without them seeing some particular evidence. In that case, say so. Skip ahead to that bit and then come back to the points they raised.

Of course, the best way to avoid having to adapt on the spot is to think about your audience and the time they have allocated for your presentation ahead of the board meeting. Company boards have heavy agendas and the firm's directors are very busy people. Your presentation will probably be one of many on the day. If they have given you 15 minutes, you'd better be 15 minutes. (Never overstay your welcome – it's rude, makes you look unprepared and won't get you the plaudits or the decision outcome you want.) That means you need to get to the point, fast.

Adapt your pace or style. It may be that your style of presenting is not hitting the mark with your audience, and you need to change. Fast. Maybe your energy is low and you're speaking in a monotone – lift your body and voice with more enthusiasm and vocal range. Or maybe it's time for your 'belly voice' – go deeper, slow it down and make the audience pay attention. Step forward to get closer to the audience. Make sure you're keeping eye contact. If you've been sitting down and talking informally, stand up. If you're using dry humour in an attempt to be lighthearted, but all your attempts at humour are whooshing over the audience's heads, revert to delivering it straight. Dry or deadpan humour is a cruel mistress. It can come over as sincere – in which case you can end up sounding rather sad or a loser – or as sarcastic and arrogant.

Whatever you do, do something – adjust, change the dynamic and go again.

Make sure you're understood. So often in business, and at home, we are in 'transmit' mode. We are so busy focusing on what we want to say that, once we've said it, we think 'job done' and expect our audience to go forth with new insight and understanding. Big mistake. It's only when nothing changes, or worse, you hear negative mutterings on the grapevine, that you realise your message/ request/*cri de coeur* must have disappeared into a big black hole.

This is particularly relevant when you're presenting internally to a board or management team and you need them to make a decision. You can't be passive – you need to ask your audience to react in order to verify misunderstandings and to get their buy-in too. Ask specific questions and don't shy away from the hard ones:

- How easy or difficult do you think this will be?
- What will get in the way of making this a reality?
- What needs to change within the company to make this happen?
- Who else needs to be brought on board in order to move to action?
- When can we start?

Go into your presentation knowing the questions that you need to have answered in order to gain understanding, support and approval. Otherwise, you're just sharing information for no purpose. Don't waste your – or their – time!

Essentially, your job is to read the signals with more confidence and react more effectively. It's an advanced skill but can be honed over time so you can adapt what you're saying, how you say it and change the emphasis as you go.

ENERGY – A CAUTIONARY TALE

It's the night before my presentation. Perhaps I'm due to deliver the keynote speech at a conference. Perhaps it's the big pitch to a prospective client I've been chasing for the past 18 months. Or perhaps I'm due to make a speech in front of my company or team and I have to deliver some bad news. Either way, I'm half dreading it, half can't wait for it to happen because currently it's all I can think about and my mind is churning as I run through all the things that could possibly go wrong.

These include:

- Failing to set my alarm and over-sleeping so I am either late or miss my slot entirely
- Forgetting my laptop with the presentation on it
- Tripping over something and falling onto the stage in the manner of Jennifer Lawrence at the Oscars only not looking quite so elegant
- Forgetting every single word of my speech
- Being heckled by the audience
- Being booed off-stage
- And on, and on

I used to spend hours mentally spiralling through a list of disasters that could potentially happen, but now, after a couple of decades of presenting where none of these things have happened, I trust the process and use my negative checklist as a spooky superstitious approach – if I have thought of all the things that could possibly go wrong then I can be confident they won't. It's usually the things I haven't thought of – the unexpected – that trip me up.

Ultimately, this final tale is less cautionary, more counsel. Instead of imagining all that could go wrong, visualise success. Visualisation is a technique that many professional athletes use – they imagine themselves on the Olympic podium and get rid of the mental negativity that may get in the way of them believing they can do it. If it works for Mo Farah, it can work for you.

Picture yourself confidently delivering your presentation. Visualise yourself speaking with clarity, confidence and enthusiasm. See your audience engaged and receptive to your message. Imagine the positive reactions you hope to receive. Visualise the applause, positive feedback, or the sense of accomplishment you will feel afterward.

Of course, this assumes you've done all the necessary preparation and rehearsal, otherwise it's less visualisation and more daydreaming. But, as Ted Lasso would say, 'Believe!'

7.
Content creation

'The difference between the right word and the almost right word is the difference between lightning and a lightning bug.'
MARK TWAIN

VISUAL AIDS

Every day we have coherent conversations with work colleagues, friends and family without having a slide presentation gently playing over our shoulder. And yet, many of us feel exposed if we present without slides, fearing we will come across as ill-prepared and lacking in intelligence if we dare to speak without having reams of data and detail on every slide. It makes no logical sense and yet we still continue with the crutch of 'visual aids'.

The very phrase, 'visual aids' sounds like it has come from a corporate training day in the mid-eighties, but how else to describe the images, pictures, video and graphics that you will use to help drive home your message? Visual storytelling? Let's go with that.

The default for many of us is to use presentation tools such as PowerPoint or Canva and then populate the slides with lines of words as a proxy for 'visuals'. The slides are then used by the presenter as a script or a prompt, often involving a lot of head turning to check the words are still up on the screen so the audience has a great view of the back of the presenter's head. The trouble is, not only is a lot of words on a screen not visually attractive, but your audience can read those words faster than they can listen to you speaking them. On average, you can listen to 125–150 words in a minute but you can read 238–300 words in the same time. So there is no point in putting your script up on the screen and expecting the audience to wait for you to plough through it – they're ahead of you already.

Ask yourself, am I using loads of busy slides because:

- It's what my company does and I don't want to be different?
- I need people to see that I have done a lot of preparation and have all the details to prove it?

Just because presentations have historically been given in a particular way at your company that doesn't mean you have to follow suit. Be the change you want to see. Make the decision today to do it a different way.

That said, there are many businesses for which people need to communicate very technical information and lots of data. I recently saw a deck of ninety-seven slides all crammed with hard-to-read data, complex graphics and no sense of structure – just slide after slide of numbers. This particular deck was heading to the CEO who would not have the time to listen to all that information but needed to know the key points. So, in this case, I advised creating a top line executive summary document for the boss, and keeping the ninety-seven data slides for the subject matter experts who – peer to peer – love discussing charts and graphics, and are happy to plough through very detailed spreadsheets.

Even so, you can still help your audience and their eyesight by not cramming teeny tiny numbers in miniscule font size onto busy slides that are impossible to read. Help your audience navigate through each slide (and the rest of the deck):

- Start with the end in mind. Be clear upfront about what you will cover, what's important for the audience to note and what you need from them at the end of your presentation
- Have a maximum of two charts per slide

- Ensure the axes are clearly labelled and easy to read
- If there's a key statistic that needs attention, put it in bold or create a callout box. (It sounds so obvious, but you cannot imagine the number of presentations I've seen that show a dense mass of numbers with no indication of what's important and what's not)
- Share the document in advance so people have a chance to read it at their own pace and then come to you with any questions. In Japanese business culture this is the norm. A *ringi* is a circulating proposal document. Any issue to be decided is summarised in such a document, which is then routed to key decision-makers. Similarly, Amazon starts every leadership meeting with 15 minutes of silence. Those minutes are filled by the people in the meeting reading any relevant papers prior to discussion. PowerPoint slides are banned at the company. You could save yourself a lot of angst and time by adopting these ideas!

Whether you're including a lot of data and charts or not, you will always need to plan your presentation first and then question whether you need visuals to help the message. And then question *if* and *where* they should go. The focus should be on YOU; you are your best visual. You can give your audience a 'leave behind' – the document with all the detail in – as you focus on communicating the salient points. Your audience is there to learn from *your* experience and expertise. If you don't add value, you can email the document and save yourself the travel time.

At all times you should be ready and able to present with no visuals. If the AV equipment doesn't work, if the PowerPoint slides are corrupt and the share screen is resolutely blank, you need to calmly demonstrate that you can carry on regardless. But in the meantime, judicious use of visual aids can provide an interesting backdrop to your speech. As we know, colour, imagery, imagination and the senses live in the right side of the brain, so if we want our message to be remembered, a well-chosen image can be incredibly helpful.

TOP TIPS

LEAD WITH AN IMAGE
If possible, have no words at all. If this is not possible, keep the words to a minimum – a pithy phrase, an arresting headline, three bullet points.

KEEP FIGURES CLEAR AND STRIKING
Round off figures to make them easier to digest and remember. It's not $3,995.689, it's $4,000,000.

TABLES OF FIGURES ARE IMPOSSIBLE TO READ AND RARELY GRAB THE AUDIENCE'S ATTENTION
Convert figures to pie charts and graphs, and pull out key statistics where you need the audience to focus. Use diagrams and flowcharts to illustrate processes, hierarchies or organisational structures. Tools like Visio or Lucidchart can help create professional diagrams.

MAKE SURE THAT YOUR LETTERS ARE BIG ENOUGH TO BE READ FROM A DISTANCE AND THAT YOU HAVE ADEQUATE SPACING
Sounds obvious but this often gets overlooked. This is why it's important to know where you are presenting. Think from the perspective of the audience member who will be furthest from the screen. Choose your point size accordingly.

Even for online presentations, allow for how your audience might be viewing what you share on screen. If they have your charts plus images of the meeting attendees too, your charts will appear small. Make them less dense and easy to read or understand. Use bullet points to share headline words rather than dense text and tables of numbers.

BE CREATIVE

Don't include the first few images you found on Google search; if they were easy for you to find, it's likely your audience will have seen them before too. Remember, beware of stock imagery. A few seconds extra to dig deeper and find a more original image – including one of your own because personal is always interesting – will pay dividends. The same goes for metaphors, analogies and examples. Avoid the well known, the familiar, the clichés. Reach for something original.

HAVE A THEME

Lots of different images that bear no relation to each other can feel disjointed and aesthetically displeasing. Explore using different images from the same source, such as one photographer (pay them and credit them!) or royalty-free images from museum or gallery online archives. If you are good, or even adequate at art, can you draw simple diagrams or cartoons to illustrate your points? And use only one image per slide. Multiple images end up being too small to see and the viewer doesn't know where to look. Your slides also end up looking a mess.

KEEP THE QUALITY

We live in a visual world, surrounded by static and moving images on our screens at all times. When your audience is looking at you and your screen, there's the expectation that it will be of the same standard as cinema, or at least YouTube or TikTok – don't let your audience down.

CONTAGIOUS MESSAGES

Contagious messages catch on and get repeated, often becoming part of people's everyday lexicon long after the advertising campaign, television programme or comic routine has ended. Decades on, people who weren't born when the **I Love New York (I ♥ NY)** slogan was created will still recognise it and use it. And it's the same for political statements that hit a nerve – love them or loathe them. The notorious Brexit slogans, 'Take back control' and 'Get Brexit done' were, fortunately or unfortunately depending on your perspective, very effective.

During his presidency, Donald Trump was criticised for the many derisive monikers he gave to his opponents. But the nicknames he gave to Hillary Clinton – 'Crooked Hillary'; Jeb Bush – 'Low energy Jeb'; and North Korean leader Kim Jong Un – 'Little Rocket Man' – fired up his support base and planted seeds of doubt about his opponents' credibility. According to Brad Bannon, a Democratic strategist, the nicknames really worked for Trump. 'They're not only an attempt to diminish an opponent, they are code words for something else. And they distract people's attention. Trump realises campaigns, especially for president, aren't about issues – they're all about personalities, especially for independent voters.'

Be they positive ('I love New York') or negative ('Lock her up'), these types of messages are memorable because of their simplicity and often because they highlight an emotion that's right on the zeitgeist. Back when outsourced call centres were starting to become big business, one of my clients quoted Blake, describing them in a speech as 'dark satanic mills' – a phrase that was picked up by the media and used for years.

If your presentation has a call to action, can you create a contagious message that will stick in people's minds? You don't need to be an advertising copywriter or a stand-up comedian to make this work for you. Sometimes messages are created organically within an organisation or within your team and you can steal them with pride.

For example, in the world of sales, there are plenty of messages that get some fundamental truths over in a short and pithy way:

– Stop selling and start helping
– There are no customers in the office
– People buy from people they like. And people generally like people who are like them
– Nothing happens until someone sells something

Here are some questions to ask yourself to help develop your own contagious message. When you're working through this process, try and be as deliberately extreme and emotive as possible. As Alex Osborn, thought to be the inventor of the word 'brainstorm', said, 'It is easier to tone down a wild idea than to think up a new one.'

- What is the emotion you want to convey? Or the emotion behind the idea?
- If you were Apple, Google, Elon Musk, PETA, Extinction Rebellion, Mary Portas, what would you say?
- Which campaign slogans inspire you? What do they do that you like? (e.g., alliteration, a rallying cry, controversy, a one-word sign off?)
- Can you express your idea in three words (rule of three)?
- What's the call to action?
- Do you believe it? Do you want to share it?
- What do other people think? Ask them

USING ARTIFICIAL INTELLIGENCE (AI)

AI, or artificial intelligence, refers to the simulation of human intelligence in machines that are programmed to think and learn like humans. It involves the development of computer systems and software that can perform tasks that typically require human intelligence, such as problem-solving, pattern recognition, language understanding and decision-making. When it comes to presentations, AI has the potential to be a massive help in terms of both the visual look of our slides and the content we wish to share.

AI-powered tools can significantly enhance presentations by automating various tasks, improving content quality and providing valuable insights. However, the world of AI is developing rapidly with new tools and applications frequently being introduced as, 'the next big thing'. Meanwhile AI tools that are seen as 'established' can quickly go out of fashion (or out of business). The list below provides the most helpful tools at the time of writing. The key thing is to work out what you need help with – for example, is it content generation or is it slide design? – and then use the list below as a starting point to find the tools that can help you. Put any of these names into Google and a host of similar applications will pop up so you can compare each one and find the best tool for your needs.

Content generation and summarisation:
- GPT-3 and GPT-4: These advanced language models can generate written content, including speeches, summaries and slides.
- Copy.ai: An AI-powered writing assistant that helps create content for presentations, including taglines, product descriptions and more.

Design and visual enhancement:
- Canva: Canva's AI-powered features assist in creating visually appealing slides and graphics, suggesting layouts, colour schemes and image recommendations.
- Visme: Offers AI design recommendations to improve the aesthetics of your presentations.

Speech and voice enhancement:
- Descript: An AI-based transcription and audio editing tool that can help clean up audio recordings and generate transcripts for your presentations.
- iSpeech: An AI text-to-speech converter that can transform written content into natural-sounding spoken words for narration.

Language translation:
- Google Translate: Utilise AI-powered translation tools to communicate with international audiences by providing real-time language translations during your presentation.

Visual content creation:
- Lumen5: An AI-powered video creation platform that can turn text-based content into engaging video presentations.
- Crello: Crello's AI tools assist in designing animated presentations, social media posts and graphics.

Data analysis and visualisation:
- Tableau: While not AI itself, Tableau can be integrated with AI and machine learning tools to create interactive and insightful data visualisations for presentations.
- Power BI: Microsoft's Power BI uses AI to analyse and present data in an easily understandable format.

Presentation coaching:
- Rehearsal: An AI-driven presentation coaching platform that provides feedback on your delivery, pacing and body language.
- VirtualSpeech: Offers AI-powered virtual reality

scenarios to practise public speaking and improve presentation skills.

Audience engagement:

- Mentimeter: Use AI polling and interactive features to engage your audience and gather real-time feedback during your presentation.
- Glisser: An AI-enhanced audience engagement platform that allows attendees to interact with your presentation using their devices.

Speech recognition and transcription:

- Otter.ai: Provides AI-driven speech recognition and transcription services, useful for capturing spoken content during presentations.
- Rev: Offers AI-powered transcription and captioning services to make your presentation content accessible.

Presentation analytics:

- Zoho Show: Provides AI-driven analytics to track audience engagement and gather insights into how your presentation is performing.

Content recommendations:

- ClearSlide: Offers AI-powered content recommendations to help you select the most effective materials for your presentation.

IMPORTANT WATCH-OUTS:

(a) Remember to evaluate the specific needs of your presentation and your audience before choosing AI tools. While AI can be a valuable resource, it's essential to use it in a way that enhances your message and presentation rather than overshadowing it.

(b) Beware of three weaknesses AI suffers from in particular. AI can help you research your presentation content, synthesise data and posit conclusions. It can save you aeons scrolling through documents, papers, reports and interview transcripts. However:

(i) AI platforms have been known to make factual errors and can suffer from the bias of the content they incorporate. So double check the main conclusions you decide to use if they have come from AI sources.

(ii) Data privacy. If you feed confidential company or personal information into an AI platform, that data is then embedded in the internet and is part of all the data sources that other AI platforms trawl on a specific subject search. Many executives have got into deep trouble by expediently saving time and effort at the cost of company confidentiality, especially by feeding in financial information.

(iii) Originality. AI platforms that can write your presentation save you lots of time. But they can make your words sound overly familiar, vanilla and, often, clichéd. AI relies on predictive text, which, as the name suggests, looks for predictable sequences of words. It pulls from massive swathes of data. But the problem is that most AI writing is fluffy and boring. Which will potentially make your presentation sound like that, too.

8.
What to wear

'The way you present yourself speaks volumes about your message.'
SILVIA DUCKWORTH

Before she retired, my mother was an art historian and often worked at the National Gallery in London. One day she was giving a lecture about Italian art in the Renaissance to a group of American visitors. They had stopped in front of five or six paintings to hear more about the historical context, the use of symbols and symmetry and the role of the Medici family in Florence. It was a well-researched presentation, delivered with enthusiasm and expertise. At the end, my mother drew to a close and said, 'Has anyone got any questions?' A hand shot up. 'Yes. Where did you get your cardigan?'

We'd all like to think that the message we want to convey is more important than the clothes we wear. However, 'the medium is the message' – if your appearance is distracting to your audience, then that is what they will focus on, not on what you are saying.

When I worked in a communications company, I had a 'pitch dress'. It was, inevitably, black. It had some interesting pleated details and, when paired with an incredibly high pair of heels (it was the 2000s), gave – I thought – the right message of *style meets business*. It also meant I didn't have to think about finding something new each time we pitched, which was one less decision to make during a fairly stressful process.

Appearance is critically important when you are representing yourself or your company. You want to feel at ease in the clothes you wear, but also use them to give you an edge – to feel you are putting on the equivalent of a superhero suit that will transform you into the best version of yourself.

I'm not going to give you guidance for what to wear in the office, in school or on the stage, as you will be aware of what works best for the culture – if you wear a suit and tie to work every day, then chances are you should do the same for your speech. If you are more comfortable in an eye-catching dress, then that's what you should choose. One piece of sartorial advice that I know some male colleagues find useful is: would James Bond wear this? If he wouldn't, perhaps you shouldn't. That said, fortunately even the corporate world is more flexible and inclusive than it was. Tattoos, piercings, clothes that express your personality are no longer as taboo as they once were. As always, start with the audience and work back from that – what do you think is both appropriate for your audience and will allow you to express the sartorial essence of you? One of my clients told the story of how he and his team turned up to a pitch during a summer heatwave wearing shorts and t-shirts, despite them all working for a big global real estate organisation that had a reputation for being corporate. 'We were pitching to a fast-growth fintech company on the hottest day of the year. We would have looked ridiculous turning up in suits and ties. I'm convinced that having the confidence to wear shorts won us that pitch.'

At the very least, be clean, be fragrant and iron your clothes.

However, should you be appearing on television or in a workplace video, what you wear has a practical application too, as certain colours are better picked up by the camera than others.

TOP TIPS FOR TELEVISION

FOR WOMEN

- **Wear solid colours.** Bright solid colours work best and contrasting colours (a green shirt under a blue jacket) work particularly well on camera. You can wear monochrome, but colour adds some 'punch', plus there's a lot of theory about how particular colours can make you feel. You may think that's a bit woo woo but if it helps, why not?

- **Avoid busy patterns and animal print.** Leave the leopard print at home as it can look distorted on camera.

- **Keep jewellery to a minimum.** Things to avoid: jangly, dangling earrings, long pendants, 'statement' necklaces, noisy bracelets. Avoid anything that could move around if you start gesturing and could interfere with the microphone. Many of us have a tendency to fiddle with our jewellery when we are nervous, which is distracting to the viewer.

- **Wear some make-up but don't trowel it on.** The myth of high-definition television is that you need heavy make-up as the cameras expose every little detail. Not so. You actually need to wear less. Yes, high-definition cameras can expose wrinkles and blemishes (AKA reality) but they also expose unnatural layers of make-up. If you're going to be a regular guest on the breakfast sofa, invest in some 'made-for-TV' cosmetic products, which are more sheer and designed to hide minor blemishes and uneven skin texture. But for one-off appearances, trust the television make-up artists to help you on the day.

- **Focus on looking comfortable.** Be very aware of your body language, because it is going to come across loud and clear. Make sure you are doing nothing distracting such as fidgeting, playing with your necklace, twisting your hair, etc. Sit back in your chair (think of the acronym BBC – bum back in chair) and cross one leg over at the ankle. Rest your arms lightly on the chair or, if there is one, the desk. Avoid taking a 'prop' such as a pen (what are you going to write?!) as it's just another thing to fiddle with.

- **Breathe.** Just before the camera turns to you, take a big breath and lower your shoulders. Think to yourself, 'I am composed. I am ready.'

FOR MEN

- **Keep to your usual style.** If you like wearing a suit, wear one. If you prefer the open-neck shirt and chinos vibe, go for that. You don't need to wear a branded polo shirt unless that's your work uniform and you want to. Unless you are on television in a personal capacity, it's likely that you are representing your organisation and therefore you need to be mindful of what's appropriate for that.

- **Choose blue.** It's a popular colour for television because it always looks good on camera. Avoid your favourite white shirt as it glows under the harsh studio lights. Red is another no-no as it bleeds out on a TV screen. If in doubt, pick subdued colours. It sounds dull but you want the audience to focus on what you're saying, not what you look like.

- **Avoid patterns** such as striped or herringbone suits but, if you're wearing one, a tie is where you can add some self-expression. Big bold patterned ties, and even large stripes do come across well on camera (but only if the rest of the outfit is solid-colour and subdued). Keep your collection of comedy ties for the office Christmas party.

- **Go for some make-up**. It's less about evening out your skin tone (although this is a benefit), it's more about avoiding a shiny, sweaty face with some judicious use of powder. If you don't have the luxury of the television programme's make-up artist, you can go to Boots and buy some foundation and powder and apply *lightly*. No need for Kim Kardashian-style contouring, just some light cover-up to avoid the shine.

Conclusion

If you picked up this book because you were one of the people who would rather die than give a presentation, I hope that I have managed to convince you that such an extreme reaction is quite unnecessary. And if you are someone who regularly gives presentations but was looking for some new inspiration and top tips, then I hope you found what you were looking for, too.

Everyone who ever stands on a conference stage, shares a presentation on Zoom or Teams, or loads their laptop with a 'deck' to share with their team, started out as a novice. Some stayed as a novice. But not you. The very fact you've picked up this book marks you out as someone who wants to improve, who's willing to put in the time and practice to get better. Take every opportunity to say 'yes' to speaking in front of an audience. Take the PRIME approach to make life easier for yourself and you will captivate, educate and inspire your audience.

As you venture forth, keep in mind these fundamental principles:

PREPARATION IS KEY
Behind every seamless presentation lies a foundation of thorough preparation. Invest time in understanding your audience, structuring your content and rehearsing your delivery. The more you prepare, the more confident and in control you'll feel on stage.

DON'T GIVE A PRESENTATION, TELL A STORY
Human beings are wired for stories. Incorporating relatable

anecdotes, examples and a clear narrative arc will make your message memorable and engaging. Craft your presentations to evoke emotions and connect with your listeners on a deeper level.

USE VISUALS TO ENHANCE UNDERSTANDING

Visual aids can transform complex concepts into easily digestible information. Use slides and other visuals judiciously to complement your spoken words. Remember, simplicity and clarity are key – too much clutter can detract from your message.

PRACTICE MAKES PERFECT

Just as musicians hone their skills through practice, so too must presenters. Rehearse your presentation multiple times. Focus on refining your tone, pacing and body language. Consider recording yourself to identify areas for improvement.

ADAPT IN THE MOMENT

No presentation unfolds exactly as planned. Embrace adaptability and be ready to adjust if needed. Flexibility shows your expertise and composure, even in challenging situations.

GET FEEDBACK

Seek feedback from trusted colleagues, mentors or even from your audience. Use constructive criticism to refine your skills and eliminate blind spots but always trust your instincts – if you don't think the feedback or advice is 'you' then feel free to ignore it. Don't try to be a Dolly Parton!

CONFIDENCE COMES WITH KNOWLEDGE

True confidence stems from knowing your material inside out. Trust that you have expertise on the subject matter to answer questions and address concerns with ease.

AUTHENTICITY CONNECTS

The most impactful presenters are authentic and genuine. Embrace your unique style and personality – your authenticity will resonate far more than trying to mimic someone else's approach.

NERVES ARE NORMAL

As you step onto the stage, remember that nerves are normal. Embrace them as a sign that you're stepping out of your comfort zone and into the realm of 'personal growth'. With each presentation, you'll refine your skills, gain confidence and build a repertoire of experiences that contribute to your success.

Finally, remember that your ability to communicate effectively is a skill that extends far beyond the conference room or Teams screen – it's a tool that can influence change, inspire action and leave a lasting impact. So, don't dread presentations, look forward to them. May your efforts be a reflection of your passion, expertise and commitment to ensuring your audience never has to sit through a boring presentation ever again.

Index